Berlitz®
USA

Original text by Jack Altman
Updated and edited by Martha Ellen Zenfell
Cover photograph by Corbis
Layout Concept: Klaus Geisler
Picture Editor: Hilary Genin
Managing Editor: Tony Halliday

D0882565

Berlitz® POCKET GUIDE

USA

Fifth Edition 2003. Updated 2005

NO part of this book may be reproduced, stored in a retrieval system or transmitted in any form or means electronic, mechanical, photocopying, recording or otherwise, without prior written permission from Berlitz Publishing. Brief text quotations with use of photographs are exempted for book review purposes only.

PHOTOGRAPHY BY:

AKG-Images London 16, 27; Pete Bennett 128; Bruce Bernstein Collection/courtesy Princeton University Library 25; Chris Coe 20, 71, 75, 76, 78, 82, 170, 174, 175; Jon Davison 81, 126, 227; Alex Demyan 14, 123, 222; Jerry Dennis 192, 200; ©Disney 188; courtesy Everglades National Park 113; Jay Fechtman 47, 49, 53, 59, 92, 97, 132, 220, 226; Glyn Genin 8, 17, 40, 111, 129, 134, 137, 166, 167, 172, 173, 176, 177, 179, 182, 183, 185, 190, 193, 211, 221, 229; GMCVB 208; GNOTCC124; Blaine Harrington 13, 140–1, 147, 148, 207; LACVB 182, 183; Las Vegas News Bureau 31, 196, 197, 198; Anna Mockford/Nick Bonetti 12, 15, 43, 45, 51, 54, 55, 56, 61, 63, 65, 66; Richard Nowitz 87, 89, 95, 98, 100, 102, 117, 118, 119, 218; Tony Perrottet 44, 52, 225; Mark Read 6, 10, 11, 84, 109, 203, 204, 209; Topham Picturepoint 32, 34, 35, 37; Doug Traverso 180, 195; Philip Ulanowsky 18.

CONTACTING THE EDITORS

Every effort has been made to provide accurate information in this publication, but changes are inevitable. The publisher cannot be responsible for any resulting loss, inconvenience or injury. We would appreciate it if readers would call our attention to any errors or outdated information by contacting Berlitz Publishing, PO Box 7910, London SE1 1WE, England. Fax: (44) 20 7403 0290; berlitz@apaguide.co.uk; www.berlitzpublishing.com

All Rights Reserved

© 2005 Berlitz Publishing/Apa Publications GmbH & Co. Verlag KG, Singapore Branch, Singapore

Printed in Singapore by Insight Print Services (Pte) Ltd, 38 Joo Koon Road, Singapore 628990.
Tel: (65) 6865-1600. Fax: (65) 6861-6438

Berlitz Trademark Reg. U.S. Patent Office and other countries. Marca Registrada

◄ New Orleans (page 121), on the Mississippi, renowned for its jazz, Mardi Gras carnival, Creole cooking and elegant colonial-style architecture

► Yosemite National Park (page 190) offers some of California's most impressive scenery, including the awesome face of 'El Capitan'

Miami Beach (page 106), destination of sunseekers and home to fine art deco architecture ▲

Washington, DC (page 84), is packed with the historic monuments of US history, as well as some fine museum ◄

TOP TEN ATTRACTIONS

The Grand Canyon (page 161), simply one of the greatest spectacles of nature on earth

Las Vegas (page 194), a city built on gambling but now offering much more with its astonishing theme hotels and spectacular shows

Los Angeles (page 180), home to Tinseltown and as much a state of mind as a city

New York City (page 41) still exerts its unique magnetism

San Francisco (page 166), one of America's favorite cities, a vibrant melting pot with a stunning natural setting and the glorious Golden Gate Bridge

Colonial Virginia (page 101), where American history was made

CONTENTS

Fact Sheets

AMERICA AND ITS PEOPLE

The United States of America is still the 'New World' for anyone who hasn't visited here before. From the beckoning beacon of the Statue of Liberty in New York, all the way across the nation to the shiny-new palaces of technology in Seattle and California, America boldly leads the world into the 21st century.

Although a trip to the USA can take in some of the world's greatest waterfalls, ski resorts, coasts, deserts, and natural wonders, one striking facet of the inhabited parts of the States is the galloping pace of newness. Still a familiar greeting all over the United States is 'Hey, what's new?' New styles and forms of recreation are limitless in the playgrounds of Miami, Los Angeles, and Las Vegas. Experiments in social organization are in evidence from New York to Washington, DC, to San Francisco. Nobody knows better than Americans that all work and no play makes for a dull population, and so the United States is also the natural home of blue jeans, tee shirts, fast food, surfboards, and rollerblades.

Change and Progress

Change and progress are more than embraced here; they are craved and pursued. In almost every city, residential areas with architectural styles up to a hundred years old surround the tall, gleaming pinnacles of downtown high-rise commercial districts. The diners and main streets of small-town USA seem to remain in a romantic time-warp somewhere around the rock & roll era of the 1950s, until suddenly you notice that everybody is communicating on cellphones, and arranging their diaries on hand-held personal computers. Cars – big and outrageous or sleek and petite – are a wonder to behold. Not only that, but gas is inexpensive.

Left, Washington, DC's Capitol building is the seat of US government

Yet some of the world's oldest, and greatest, natural phenomena are on display in forms as diverse as the vast Grand Canyon, white-hot Death Valley, shimmering Niagara Falls, the glorious Great Lakes, national parks of every conceivable description, and that 'Old Man River' itself, the mighty Mississippi that traverses most of the country from north to south.

Geography

With an area of approximately 3,717,700 sq. miles (9,629,000 sq. km), including Alaska and Hawaii, the US is the fourth largest country in the world, or nearly 40 times the size of the UK. Mainland USA (excluding Alaska and Hawaii), called the 48 contiguous states, stretches for about 3,000 miles (4,800km) from the Atlantic to the Pacific and for some 1,200 miles (1,900km) from the Canadian border to the Gulf of Mexico.

The largest state in the union is Alaska, nearly 152,000 sq. miles (1.4m sq. km). Hawaii, the 50th state, is located in the Pacific Ocean, some 2,500 miles (4,000km) to the southwest. The highest point is the summit of Mt McKinley (Alaska), 20,320ft (6,194m). The lowest point is in 282ft (86m) below sea level in Death Valley (California), the second lowest point on dry land anywhere in the world.

Hawaiian beach life

Government and Population

The US is a federal republic consisting of 50 states and one federal district (Washington's District of Columbia – the 'DC' of the name). There is a two-party political system (the Democrats and the Republicans). The government is based on the Consti-

Maritime history - the *USS Constitution* in Boston

tution of 1787. The president is elected for a period of 4 years, and can be re-elected once. The Congress is composed of the Senate (with two senators per state) and the House of Representatives (435 members, proportionately drawn from the states according to their population).

Each state has its own semiautonomous government and local laws, headed by a popularly elected governor. The population of 282 million is made up of 82.2 percent whites, 12.8 percent African-Americans, 1 percent Native Americans, and 4 percent of other races. Religions according to the census are 56 percent Protestant, 28 percent Roman Catholic, 2 percent Jewish, 4 percent other, 10 percent none.

Culture

Other countries display their glorious past in museums, cathedrals, temples, and palaces. America shows off and shares its exuberant present – but in the street and on the beach. Other countries talk of their culture; America welcomes visitors to its way of life. The days when Europeans might hazard a patronizing observation on America's cultural life should be well and truly over by now. In fields like classical music, opera, and the visual arts, the United States can give a good account of itself in any company.

The Arts

America is home to seven world-famous symphony orchestras and opera companies in Chicago, New York, Los Angeles, Philadelphia, Cleveland, Washington, DC, and Boston. The endlessly innovative paintings and sculptures of Manhattan and California are regularly featured among the world's leading art movements.

The great museums of New York, Washington, and Chicago stand among the world's finest. Nationwide, American architecture is forever seeking and finding novel solutions, contributing to the inspirational traditions from Frank Lloyd Wright to Frank Gehry.

Art and architecture: inside New York's Guggenheim Museum

The architecture of America is often superb, occasionally startling, but never timid, addressing the problems of urban working and living space in an overcrowded age.

The Great Outdoors

Americans were clearly the spoiled children of creation when it came to distributing the bounty of the earth, and have in their easy reach a fantastic diversity of landscapes to which they can escape.

Winter sports in Colorado

The country's environmental reawakening started just in time to preserve much of the natural beauty of the continent's wide open spaces.

For sailors and anyone who likes to fish, there are the wild Atlantic coasts of Maine and Florida as well as their Pacific counterparts in northern California, Oregon, and Washington state. There are also the calmer waters of Long Island Sound and Chesapeake Bay, or the lazy beaches of the Gulf Coast and southern California. In between are the Great Lakes of the Midwest, which might easily qualify as seas anywhere else in the world.

National Parks

Throughout the country are great national parks and nature reserves, luring visitors to hike around the swamps of Florida's Everglades and climb in the White Mountains of New Hampshire, the Great Smokies of North Carolina and Tennessee, or the Rockies of Colorado. The vast parks of the West, with the geysers, waterfalls, and evergreen forest of Wyoming's Yellowstone; the rainbow canyons of Utah's Zion; the massive redwoods of northern California, the stupendous rock faces of Yosemite; and of course Arizona's Grand Canyon, all offer sanctuaries in which to enjoy the natural beauty that contains the soul of this industrial giant. Even the deserts – the Petrified Forest southeast of the Grand Canyon, or Death Valley in California's Mojave – grant an enriching respite from civilization.

City Life

But civilization American-style is just too much fun to stay away from for too long. Each of the major cities offers its own adventure. The street life of New York is a carnival – endless movement, color, noise, taste, and aroma – sometimes hair-raising, always stimulating. Boston, Washington, and Philadelphia are metropolitan pillars of American history, proud and dignified towns that don't take themselves too seriously. New Orleans offers a deliciously exotic jambalaya of old elegance and decadence, part Gallic, part Deep South, but always vibrant and musical. Santa Fe is its Spanish counterpart, but quieter, more the culture of fine arts rather than the romance of jazz. There's nothing quiet or delicate about big, boisterous Chicago, however. The town never fails to surprise visitors with the beauty of its lake-front architecture, or the breadth and exhuberance of its musical heritage.

Listen to the best music at the House of Blues, New Orleans

Dallas and Houston are the bumptious concrete realizations of the Texan dream, ranchers gone oil-rich urban. Crazy Los Angeles and gorgeous, nonconformist San Francisco are the last extravagant points on the map of

Manhattan from the Empire State Building

America's push West. Big and small, America's cities are both playgrounds and workshops displaying the best, and some of the worse, aspects of a century of tireless urban development.

Fantasy Playgrounds

If you're exhausted from taking in the wonders of the real world, you can revel in the fantasy realms of Universal Studios and Disneyland, or the sinful glamour of Las Vegas and other 'theme resorts' that have burst glittering across the country. The thrills and excitement are carefully designed not to create too much stress – all good clean family fun (apart from Las Vegas, of course; Sin City obeys few rules). Children have an important place in local life, and Americans have long understood that all of us, some of the time – perhaps more often than we are willing to admit – are children.

Americans love to play. Their own versions of old European sports – baseball (which an American encyclopedia admits is 'doubtless derived' from English cricket and rounders) and what they call football, which looks to foreign

eyes like a contest that might easily have been invented for Roman gladiators – are exuberant spectacles. In addition to the spectator sports are the endless fads that spring up around the beaches of Florida, California, or Hawaii – surfing, rollerblading, parascending, and sand yachting – all come and go with the swift arc of a frisbee.

Diversity

Freedom on the road

In a country as vast and varied as the United States, it is hazardous to try and pin down the catch-all moniker of 'Americans.' White Anglo-Saxon Protestants? Irish Catholics? Hispanics, Poles, Italians, Germans, Greeks, Arabs, Scandinavians, Russians, Jews, Czechs, Africans, Chinese, Japanese, Vietnamese, or Sioux, Navajo, Cherokee, and Cheyenne? Or, for that matter, New Yorkers and New Englanders, Southerners and Texans, Midwesterners and hillbillies, and again, to confound all generalizations – Californians? It's worth making out this long and far-from-exhaustive list just to be able to contemplate the incredible diversity of these people collectively called Americans.

And then you realize that this is the answer. This is the valid definition of 'Americans;' they are this culture of boundless variety. Somehow people from every far-flung corner of the earth have ended up living together – not always peacefully by any means – but despite revolution and civil war and riots, with such astounding success.

Perhaps the greatest adventure of your American journey will be to encounter as many as you can of the different people making up these United States: the cool New Englanders, pushy New Yorkers, bluff and hearty Texans, earnest Midwestern farmers – and their exact opposites, for no generalization stands up to more than five minutes' scrutiny in this super-country.

Discovery

Wherever you discover Americans, you'll be sure to see that they have not coalesced into a dull, homogeneous nation of look-alikes, talk-alikes, and laugh-alikes. Martin Luther King, Jr, was right to contest the image of America as a melting pot. He said it was in fact a good bowl of vegetable soup in which you could taste the carrots, potatoes, leeks, and peas, all separately, and all together.

The one thing you can say for sure is that every time you visit, you'll find that the recipe has been varied, spiced, and flavored again and again.

El Capitan in California's Yosemite National Park

A BRIEF HISTORY

For at least 25,000, maybe as many as 40,000, years, at a time when mammoth and bison left Siberia for new pastures across a now submerged land bridge over the Bering Strait, North America has been inhabited by man. Mongolian hunters, probable ancestors of later Indian tribes, followed the bison into what is now the state of Alaska.

Over the centuries, some made their way down the Pacific coast and east across the continent. Between 500BC and AD500, the Hopi and Zuni settled in farming communities in adobe-walled *pueblos* of New Mexico and Arizona. By 1500, the only truly nomadic natives were the Plains Indians roaming between the Rockies and the Mississippi River forests. Tribes along the East Coast were skilled farmers, growing beans, squash, maize, and tobacco. But they had no wheel, either for wagon or pottery, no metal tools, and no horses. Their only beasts of burden were dogs.

The Europeans Arrive

The claim that the 6th-century Irish monk St Brendan got here first is a nice piece of blarney, but historians accept that Norsemen from Greenland crossed to Newfoundland between 1001 and 1015. Then they disappeared again without trace.

Not so the Spanish. It was 10pm on October 11, 1492, when the Genoese captain acting for the Spanish monarchy, Christopher Columbus, stood with his watchman looking at a pale light on the western horizon. It turned out to be on an island in the Bahamas, just 380 miles (612km) from what centuries later became Miami Beach. Although Columbus was to die almost penniless, he is the man credited with discovering America.

Five years later, another Genoese-born sailor, John Cabot, set foot in Newfoundland, stopping just long enough to stake the fateful English claim to North America for his master, Henry VII.

Left, signing the Declaration of Independence

But it was the name of a third Italian explorer, Amerigo Vespucci, that was used by a mapmaker and stuck to both northern and southern continents.

The first European contact with the future United States mainland came in 1513, when Spanish explorer Juan Ponce de León was searching for the fabled Fountain of Youth and stumbled upon the coast of Florida. In 1565, the Spaniards built a fort along at St Augustine, the first permanent settlement in North America.

The English began seriously to explore in 1607. After cursory examination (by Sir Francis Drake) of what was to become California and some unsuccessful efforts on the East Coast (by Sir Walter Raleigh), they established their first settlement at Jamestown, Virginia. Then on November 11, 1620, over a hundred people fleeing from religious persecution sighted Cape Cod, Massachusetts while aboard the *Mayflower*. The seeds of American democracy were contained in a remarkable covenant drawn up by these 'pilgrims' – the *Mayflower Compact*, which provided that laws accepted by the majority would be binding on all. They founded a community at Plymouth Bay, learning from friendly natives how to fish and plant maize. Half the pilgrims died that first hard winter. The following October, after the harvest, the survivors and 90 Wampanoag Indians held a three-day feast of wild turkey and waterfowl – the very first Thanksgiving.

The *Mayflower II* at Plymouth

In 1626, the Manhattan Indians sold their island to the Dutch West India Company for the legendary sum of $24, and New Amsterdam sprang up as a classic seaman's town of taverns and seedy hangouts for smugglers and illicit traders. Apart from a few farms, or *boweries*, the Dutch didn't invest much in their American property, concentrating their energies on the East Indies. Smart New Englanders moved down to Westchester and Long Island and the English began putting pressure on the Dutch to move out. In 1664, the English fleet in the harbor, Dutch governor, Peter Stuyvesant, let New Amsterdam become New York without a shot being fired. Some Dutch families remained, including the Roosevelts, who later went on to produce two presidents.

> **In 1681, William Penn set up a colony in Philadelphia. This energetic Quaker from London established the proprietary province of Pennsylvania as a haven of free enterprise and religious tolerance. Swedes, Finns, and Dutch already settled there were now joined by farmers from England, France, and Germany.**

Toward Revolution

As the British Empire expanded in the middle of the 18th century, London demanded that the American colonies contribute more to its upkeep and defense. While accepting London's authority in foreign affairs, the colonists assumed they would enjoy the same freedoms and privileges as other Englishmen. But between 1764 and 1767 a series of special taxes (on newspapers and legal documents) and import duties (on sugar, silk, linen, Madeira wine, paint, lead, paper, and tea) made them realize they weren't just Englishmen abroad. A South Carolina leader, Christopher Gadsden, drew the inevitable conclusion: 'There ought to be no New England men, no New Yorkers known on the continent, but all of us Americans.'

Groups known as the 'Sons of Liberty' formed in New York and Boston, attacked the royal tax collectors' houses, and burned their furniture. In Boston the propagandist and agitator Samuel Adams led dances around the Liberty Tree, an elm from which unpopular officials were hanged in effigy. As unrest mounted, the British sent two regiments to Boston. In March 1770, a mob snowballed guards in front of the Boston Customs House. The attack grew fiercer and the British fired, killing four Bostonians.

Boston Tea Party

Most of the offending duties repealed, there followed three years of peace and prosperity. But the duty on tea remained. While Philadelphia and New York staged boycotts, Sam Adams's Sons of Liberty (disguised as Mohawk Indians) boarded three British ships in Boston Harbor and dumped the cargo in the sea. The Boston Tea Party of 1773 moved George III to say: 'The colonies must either submit or triumph.' The Americans agreed.

The American colonies called their First Continental Congress in Philadelphia in September 1774 to coordinate opposition. Again, Massachusetts took the lead, declaring itself a 'free state' and preparing to resist any British offensive with weapons and ammunition stored at Concord. The British moved 12,000 troops to Boston and, in April 1775, a contingent marched out to deal with the rebels. Paul Revere, as legend has it, rode 'through every Middlesex village and farm' to warn of the British advance on Concord. The first resistance was at Lexington, but it was on the bridge at Concord that 'embattled farmers' faced the British and 'fired the shot heard round the world.'

Declaration of Independence

Despite the Second Continental Congress's push for independence – led by Massachusetts' John Hancock, Virginia's Thomas Jefferson, and Pennsylvania's Benjamin Franklin – many were still reluctant to sever the ties with Britain. Within a few months, though, they moved 'That these United Colonies are, and of right ought to be, Free and Independent States.' On July 4, 1776, the Declaration of Independence was signed, proclaiming 'life, liberty and the pursuit of happiness' the aim of the United States of America's government.

The war dragged on for seven more years, patriot farmers engaging the British in skirmishes, in a morale-sapping battle of strategic attrition. After the Battle of Long Island in August 1776, the British took control of New York for the rest of the war. Philadelphia fell in September 1777, leaving Washington and his depleted forces to shiver out the winter in nearby Valley Forge.

The British assumed control of the Atlantic coast, gaining victories at Savannah and Charleston. Then American troops forged north to Virginia, picking off British outposts along the way. There, French support paid off in a combined action with Washington in which 15,000 men won the decisive Battle of Yorktown. On October 17, 1781, Lord Cornwallis's British soldiers surrendered. After two years of tedious negotiations led by Benjamin Franklin, the Peace of Paris ended the war on September 3, 1783.

The New Republic Expands Westward

New York was the first capital of the new United States of America, and it was on a balcony overlooking Wall Street on April 30, 1789, that George Washington was inaugurated as president. Endowed with great character, he made up for his lack of political talent by surrounding himself with men who possessed it in abundance, among them Thomas Jefferson as secretary of state and Alexander Hamilton at the treasury. His vice-president was John Adams – cousin of Sam, the Boston Tea Party troublemaker.

As champion of a new democracy, Jefferson was disturbed by an obstacle to it on his own doorstep. The United States' first census of 1790 showed a population of nearly four million, of whom 700,000 were black slaves. Himself a slave-owner on his Virginia farm, Jefferson expressed hopes for 'a total emancipation,' fearing dire trouble for the Union of the states.

Jefferson was elected president in 1800, and early the next year was the first to be inaugurated in the new capital, the town of

Washington on the Potomac River along the eastern seaboard. Apart from the White House and the Capitol, this was little more than a collection of ramshackle boarding houses, where many senators and congressmen had to bed down on the floor.

One of the major triumphs of the Jefferson presidency was the Louisiana Purchase of 1803. The French territory stretched from the Mississippi to the Rocky Mountains, 828,000 sq. miles (2,144,520 sq. km) that more than doubled the size of the country. Preoccupied with an insurrection in Haiti and his war with the British, Napoleon was happy to sell the land for $15 million. The next year, Captain Meriwether Lewis and Lieutenant William Clark set out from St Louis to explore the uncharted West all the way to the Pacific Ocean.

The expedition was intended not only to lay American claim to the Oregon territory but also to size up the 'Indian situation' in the Northwest. Many suspected that the British were encouraging the tribes to resist American western expansion. This and disputes over free trade rights during Britain's naval blockade of Napoleon led, under President James Madison, to another war with the British, from 1812 to 1814. The US invaded Canada, killing the great tribe leader Tecumseh and burning parliamentary houses in York (later Toronto) as well as surrounding villages. The British retaliated at Fort Niagara and Buffalo. Washington was attacked and the White House set on fire.

Pushing West

Under President Andrew Jackson, the American frontier was pushed to the West. Trappers and furhunters led the new pioneers from the Missouri River to the Rockies during the 1830s. In canvas-covered wagons known as 'prairie schooners,' thousands of backwoodsmen set out for Oregon in the 1840s. America's drive to the Pacific Ocean was proclaimed to be the nation's 'manifest destiny.' Other Americans moved beyond the United States frontiers to Mexican-owned Texas. By 1836 they were 20,000 strong, outnumbering the Mexicans there by four to one. They liked Mexican horsemanship, saddles, and trappings, but rebelled against the authoritarian

Covered wagons on the Oregon Trail

government. After fierce fighting in retaliation for the Mexican massacre of Americans at the Alamo, Texas was made an independent 'Lone Star Republic.' In 1845 it was annexed to the US.

The Civil War

Throughout the era of western expansion, the slavery issue festered. Slaves made up 40 percent of the southern states' population. As long as cotton was 'king,' representing two-thirds of US exports, the South felt it could justify working slaves on the plantations. When rebellions broke out in South Carolina and Virginia, repression was ruthless, and strict curfews were placed on all African-Americans. Owners organized night patrols, and teaching slaves to read or write was strictly forbidden.

In the North, the Abolitionist movement grew to 200,000 by 1840. Since slave owners could legally reclaim fugitives in the Northern states, an 'Underground Railroad' was organized to help slaves escape north into Canada. By the 1850s, any lingering moral considerations the South may have had were blurred by the purely political issue of states' rights. The slave states insisted on the right to decide their own affairs without the interference of the federal government.

A new Republican Party was founded in 1854 on an antislavery platform and, by the 1860 presidential elections, was firmly identified with the North. The Democrats split on the issue of whether the new western territories should be obliged to permit slavery, and southern states fielded their own candidate in addition to the Democrats' official nominee. The Republicans chose a man of reassuringly simple personality who could get enough support in the new Midwestern states to guarantee victory over the divided Democrats. The homespun Illinois attorney, 'honest' Abraham Lincoln, did the trick.

South Carolina lead Mississippi, Alabama, Florida, Georgia, Louisiana, and Texas into secession from the Union. The reason was that the North had elected 'a man whose opinions and purposes are hostile to slavery.' In fact, Lincoln's aims were not so simple. As he wrote to a New York editor: 'My paramount object in this struggle is to save the Union and not either to save or destroy slavery.' But he had said earlier: 'I believe this government cannot endure permanently half *slave* and half *free*.'

In February 1861, the Confederate States of America elected as their president Jefferson Davis, an aristocratic ex-soldier. Arkansas, Tennessee, Virginia, and North Carolina joined the Confederacy, but Kentucky, after some hesitation, did not. Nor did Missouri, Maryland, or Delaware. Virginia's great military leader, General Robert E. Lee, was more ambivalent than the politicians. 'I can contemplate no greater calamity for the country,' he wrote in January 1861, 'than a dissolution of the Union. Still, a Union that can only be maintained by swords and bayonets and in which strife and civil war are to take the place of brotherly love or kindness, has no charm for me.' This troubled, noble hero promptly emancipated his slaves but joined the southern cause.

The Civil War saw the first use of an iron-clad ship, and even an experimental submarine.

On April 12, 1861, South Carolina troops opened fire

on the US military base of Fort Sumter, and the Civil War began. The four-year war was a horror. Grand moments of heroism in the battles of Antietam (Maryland), Gettysburg (Pennsylvania), Fredericksburg (Virginia), Shiloh (Tennessee), and Vicksburg (Mississippi) were mere punctuation marks, however glorious, in the cold, wet, disease-ridden guerrilla-style conflict. More than twice as

Manning the guns during the Civil War

many died from Dysentery, typhoid, malaria, and consumption as were killed by bullets and bayonets.

The South had proud military traditions, superior officers and training, but the North had overwhelming supremacy in heavy industry, railways, and arms. It triumphed despite often incompetent military leadership. While Lee brought classical elegance and Thomas 'Stonewall' Jackson a fatalistic realism to southern generalship, the North's Ulysses Grant and William Sherman demonstrated relentless willpower and brute force. After Grant occupied the Confederate capital of Richmond, Virginia, Lee submitted the South's surrender at Appomattox on April 9, 1865. Just five days later, Lincoln was assassinated at Ford's Theater in Washington by the actor and Confederate sympathizer John Wilkes Booth.

Reconstruction

Ravaged by the war, its major cities reduced to rubble, Georgia in ruin from Atlanta to Savannah, the Southern economy was shattered, its banks insolvent. The cotton crop of 1860 was not matched again till 1879. As the planter-aristocracy moved out, either to the North and West or abroad to England, Mexico, or Brazil, poor white farmers took over. The North had prospered, the war having profited a new class of millionaire – Rockefeller in oil, Remington in guns (later typewriters). Over 800,000 immigrants streamed into the North during the war and over 3 million more followed in the next 10 years.

African-Americans, 4 million freed by the Union's victory, faced more hardships. After the first euphoria they woke to the embittered South's new 'black codes' under which they could not vote, testify against whites, bear arms, or frequent public places reserved for whites. The Washington government could not make good on the '40 acres and a mule' which had been promised each freed slave. The most positive achievement of the Freedmen's Bureau was to set up new hospitals and schools. But many African-Americans also faced greater violence than they had ever known as slaves, and the Ku Klux Klan, founded in Tennessee in 1866, spread terror throughout the South.

The federal government's Reconstruction Acts replaced recalcitrant southern-state governments with Northerners and African-Americans, backed by federal troops, to guarantee 'equal protection of the laws.' However, under Rutherford Hayes, the Enforcement Acts were nullified, and for three gen-

Indian Country

The battle for the land and its riches had been waged against the Native American tribes ever since Europeans first set foot on American soil. It reached its climax after the Civil War, when the government set out to finally 'conquer' the West and force the tribes onto reservations. Despite Custer's last stand, the invasion by the white man was unstoppable, a fact well understood by Chief Joseph of the Nez Perce as he pondered the plight of his people:

'I have carried a heavy load on my back ever since I was a boy. I realized then that we could not hold our own with the white men. We were like deer. They were like grizzly bears. We had small country. Their country was large. We were contented to let things remain as the Great Spirit Chief made them. They were not, and would change the rivers and mountains if they did not suit them.'

erations southern African-Americans were in a limbo between slavery and freedom.

The World Stage

By 1914, America had established itself as the world's leading industrial power. Railroad, steel, coal, oil, and the vast agricultural resources of the Great Plains brought wealth such as had never before been witnessed.

Fresh arrivals in New York in the late 19th century

From 1860 to 1920, the population more than tripled, from 31 to 106 million. This was the period of massive immigration: four million British, four million Irish, six million Germans, over two million Scandinavians, and Italians, Poles, Czechs, Austrians, Hungarians, Serbs, and Russian Jews. Northern Europeans went West, to the farmlands; Southern and Eastern Europeans and the Irish stuck to the big Eastern and Midwestern cities. Jews went into the garment industry, Finns into the mines, Portuguese into textiles. The Chinese worked in the mines and on the railways – and suffered from anti-Oriental laws when white Americans became scared for their jobs.

The trade union movement – or organized labor, as it is known in the US – was less political than in Europe. Rather than question the virtues of the capitalist system, it demanded its share of the profits. This proved hard enough, and the strikes, lock-outs, and pitched battles between workers and company militia were as violent as any in the 'old country.'

In the imperial spirit of the times, America bought Alaska from Russia in 1867 and absorbed Hawaii by negotiating trading and military privileges with the strategically vital Pacific islands. In the Caribbean, the US proved itself adept at gunboat diplomacy.

In the 1898 war against the Spanish, America ended up in charge of Puerto Rico and Guam (in the Pacific), military occupation of the Philippines, and the role of godfather to Cuba's independence.

As the old nations fought on the battlefields of Europe, America was ready for the world stage. Woodrow Wilson, son of a southern Presbyterian minister, brought a decidedly moral and didactic flavor to the presidency. After helping the Allies to victory over Germany, Wilson presented at the Versailles peace negotiations an elaborate plan for a League of Nations. He ran into anti-German jingoism of the British and the open cynicism of France's Georges Clemenceau: 'Mr. Wilson bores me with his Fourteen Points; why, God Almighty has only ten!'

Boomtime and the Great Depression

After the Russian Revolution, America succumbed to a Red Scare. The New York state legislature expelled five socialist members because of their politics. In 1927, Bartolomeo Vanzetti and Nicola Sacco, two Italian-born anarchists charged with murdering a shoe-factory paymaster in Massachusetts, were executed. Many held that the jury was swayed more by its fear of anarchic politics than by its conviction of criminal responsibility. The 1920s were also when the good times rolled: jazz, radio, silent movies, and cars – 26 million by the end of the decade. Materialism was respectable. As President Calvin Coolidge put it: 'The business of America is business' – and it was enjoying a boom.

The growth of the big cities with their exotic immigrant populations brought a threat to the old American rural and small-town principles. Prohibition of alcohol in 1920 was justified with moral argument, but far from upholding morality, Prohibition promoted gangland crime. Federal enforcement agents went into league with hoodlum Al Capone's bootleggers.

In 1928, Herbert Hoover, a great humanitarian in World War I with a mining engineer's efficiency and very much the candidate of American business, arrived in the White House with high hopes: 'poverty will be banished from this nation.' The next year came the Great Crash of the New York Stock Exchange and

The Mob found legitimacy in early Las Vegas

America slumped into the Depression. Between 1929 and 1932, 5,000 banks closed down. One-third of the population were either unemployed by 1933, or members of families whose breadwinner was out of work. People went hungry while fruit, vegetables, and grain were in abundance. Houses were unheated while coal piled up. America was stunned by the failure of its classic virtues of business leadership, organization, and efficiency.

In 1933, Franklin D. Roosevelt embarked on a whirlwind 'Hundred Days' of economic and social measures to conquer the catastrophe. With a canny sense of public relations, the president confided in the people with radio 'fireside chats,' and cheered them up by legalizing wine and beer while Prohibition was dismantled federally and handed over to state legislation.

F.D.R.'s 'New Deal' did beat back the disaster of the Depression, but economic recession did not end till World War II.

World War II and Beyond

After Woodrow Wilson's internationalist adventures, America preferred the small comforts of isolation, coupled with a pacifist

The *Arizona* is sunk at Pearl Harbor

reaction in general. Even F.D.R. said in 1936: 'We shun political commitments which might entangle us in foreign wars.' But the neutralist policy was revoked after Hitler's 1940 *Blitzkrieg* against Belgium, France, and the Netherlands. Congress appropriated $37 million for arms and aid to its allies – but still resisted conscription. The Japanese raid on Pearl Harbor, on December 7, 1941, ended all hesitation.

Roosevelt was reelected to an unprecedented fourth term in 1944, but after a long struggle with infantile paralysis, he died in April 1945, before the final victory. Harry Truman made the decision to use an atom bomb to end the war with Japan.

After World War II, America emerged as the only major power undamaged by the conflict. In fact, the US economy had grown, and left America poised as the preeminent leader of international commerce. American corporations like Boeing and General Electric, as well as Coca-Cola and the movie business of Hollywood all had a 'good war' and came out very prosperous.

Times at home were good for most, although the inequalities and ethnic tensions in-built in the Land of the Free were set to bring domestic conflict during these 'peace years.'

Civil Rights

The 1950s were a brash, confident decade of prosperity and possibility. Cars were big, clothes were sharp, and disc jockey Alan Freed coined the term 'rock & roll' to make black rhythm and blues accessible to white audiences. One Elvis Aaron Presley stepped into Sam Phillips' Sun Studios in Memphis with a disc he'd cut in a recording booth, and from then on the world reeled each time he swiveled his hips.

Half-way through the decade, in 1955, President Eisenhower sent the first 'military advisors' to Vietnam. The same year Dr Martin Luther King, Jr led the first black bus boycott, and the next year, the Supreme Court outlawed segregation on buses. The march for black equal rights was on.

On September 2 1957, nine black students were due to start their new school year in Little Rock, Arkansas. As theirs was a newly desegregated school, fierce passions boiled around the issue, and the National Gaurd were called out to protect the school. Initially they prevented the students from entering. It took 23 days, 10,000 National Guardsmen, 1,000 paratroops, a court injunction, and the intervention of Eisenhower himself before the students were able to start lessons. The issues of desgregation and equality of citizenship rumbled on until the Civil Rights Act of 1964, with many of the scars still visible today.

> **At the end of the 1950s, the United States was still growing in size, as well as in stature. Alaska and Hawaii became the 49th and 50th states in 1959.**

The Kennedy Era

At the beginning of the 1960s, John F. Kennedy was elected president, narrowly beating Richard Nixon. After a tough time with the press in the campaign, Nixon conceeded saying, 'You won't have Nixon to push around any more.' Not his last public pronouncement that would turn out to be untrue. As a gesture of American can-do grit, President Kennedy committed the US to putting a man on the moon by the end of the decade.

Kennedy, with his brother Bobby as Attorney General, presided in dangerous times. Bobby tried to fight organized crime in the teeth of opposition from the Director of the FBI, J. Edgar Hoover. Hoover said that the real threat was from the 'enemy within,' the Red Peril (meaning Communists). Meanwhile, J.F.K. had to deal with 'real reds' just across the sea from Miami, in Fidel Castro's Cuba. Perhaps acting on poor advice, Kennedy committed 1,600 CIA trained insurgents to invade

Cuba. They were easily defeated with massive losses, and the result was known as the Bay of Pigs fiasco. Maybe emboldened, Russia stationed missiles at bases in Cuba. They were detected by American reconnaisance flights, and on April 22, 1962, Kennedy demanded them withdrawn. He mounted a naval and air blockade, and the world held its breath for six days. In exchange for a face-saving promise not to invade Cuba, Russian Premier Khrushchev backed down and removed the missiles.

With the prosperity of the 1960s, America's mood was one where the problem of how to survive seemed to have been solved. Collective thoughts now turned towards how to live. In 1962, women's rights activist and journalist Betty Friedan published *The Feminist Mystique*. She founded the National Organization for Women in 1966, but it still took until 1974 for an equal pay act from the Supreme Court. The 1960s Civil Rights movement swept the nation, as did the anti-war movement, both espoused by the hippies and flower children of California.

Love and Death

In the mid-1960s, San Francisco became the center of a hippie revolution. By 1967, the Haight-Ashbury neighborhood was thronged with long-haired young men and women promoting

Summer of Love

free love and a philosophy that basically said 'let it be,' culminating in a globally recognized 'Summer of Love.' But the 1960s was also a decade of violent political unrest. John F. Kennedy was shot dead in Dallas, Texas, on November 22, 1963. Lee Harvey Oswald was held to have been the lone assassin, but he, too, was murdered by night club owner and sometime FBI informant Jack Ruby, long

M.L.K. gives his 'I have a dream' speech, Washington, DC, 1963

before any trial could be brought. Martin Luther King, Jr was killed in Memphis, Tennessee on April 4, 1968, prompting riots in more than 100 US cities. Just a month later, Bobby Kennedy was gunned down after a campaign address in Los Angeles.

1968 was also the year in which Richard Milhouse Nixon made his second – this time successful – bid for the White House. Nixon, like his predecessors, promised an early end to American participation in the Vietnam war. Like presidents before him, he found it a tough promise to deliver. Still, Nixon was able to deliver on one of Kennedy's dreams; on July 20, 1969, Neil Armstrong stepped out of the *Apollo 11* lunar module onto the surface of the moon.

Nixon's second term of presidency was hopelessly mired in the scandal and criminal proceedings from a burglary at the Watergate building in Washington, DC. It was the vice-president, Gerald Ford, who was able to declare the final withdrawal from Vietnam on May 7, 1975. Ford has the unique distinction of having been both vice president and president of the United States, without being elected to either office. Spiro Agnew had been compelled to resign as vice president when he faced numerous charges of bribery and eventually accepted the time-honored catch-all of 'evading income tax.' Nixon appointed Ford to the vice-presidential vacancy. When Nixon himself was forced to resign over the Watergate affair, Ford took over the Oval Office.

The 1970s to 1990s

Hopeful of consigning scandals and disgrace to the past, in 1976 America chose a little-known peanut farmer from Georgia as its president. Jimmy Carter's term saw a nuclear incident at Three Mile Island and a world oil crisis. He was, however, able to establish full diplomatic relations with China, and begin a hopeful peace process for the Middle East. But Carter's presidency was marred by the taking in Tehran of around 70 American hostages. For 444 days the story was at the top of every news broadcast. Carter tried diplomacy and an abortive rescue attempt.

By coincidence, or careful plotting, depending on your point of view, the hostages were finally released on the day of Ronald Reagan's innauguration as the 40th president in 1981. In 1986, Reagan admitted having secretly sold arms to Iran in what became known as the Iran-Contra scandal.

The tenure of Reagan's vice president and successor, George Bush, was marked by the Gulf War in 1991, and still more race riots in 1992. He was also able to turn the economy around, but most of the credit went to the 42nd president, Bill Clinton.

The 1980s and 1990s saw another migration West, as thousands of Americans left the chilly winds and the uncertain economics of the East Coast to test their future on the sunny shores of California. West Coast businesses began to nurture co-operation with what became known as the 'Pacific Rim'; the West Coast of America, and the parts of Asia bordering the Pacific Ocean. Traditional Pacific Northwest industries –

> **When Ronald Reagan was wounded in an assassination attempt, he later told his wife Nancy, 'Honey, I forgot to duck'.**

lumber, agriculture and fishing – took second place to shipping and light manufacturing opportunities with Asia, kindling interest in Seattle, Washington, and Portland, Oregon. At the same time, a former orchard-filled area called the Santa Clara Valley south of San Francisco, was to be reborn as Silicon Valley.

Bill Clinton

The Rise of the Internet

Toward the end of the 20th century, American ingenuity brought a revolution to the world of commerce and communications with a legacy from the Cold War missile program. The ARPA net was a system of telephone connections that would automatically re-route to avoid any kind of damage, to ensure connections in an attack. Computer scientists in the 1980s realized that this gave them the ability to link computers almost anywhere, using public phone lines.

This was the birth of the internet, e-mail and the world wide web. The opportunity for individuals to communicate instantly and inexpensively changed the way that businesses, news-gatherers, and eventually just plain folk were able to talk, whether to someone on the other side of town or on the other side of the globe. College kids in the western edges of the old Soviet Union made contact with their peers in California and Chicago. Businesses found new customers and suppliers. Families separated by miles or oceans were able to swap news and gossip.

The American spirit of entrepreneurship saw a pot of gold at the end of the internet rainbow, and investors poured billions of dollars into thousands of dot-com dreams. Seattle, Portland, San Francisco, and the Silicon Valley boomed. Expectations rose, results were slow, and a crash was inevitable. Just as slender ideas had been over-valued, even so-solid companies were destroyed.

President Bill Clinton, too, was beset by scandal, in this case both financial and personal. The Kenneth Starr investigation was originally a probe into property and share deals from Clinton's time as governor of Arkansas, but the headlines and eventual congressional hearings became fixated on the seemingly endless parade of women in Clinton's life.

The Millinneum and Beyond

In November 2000, Clinton's vice president, Al Gore, stood against George Bush's son, George W. Bush. The ballot was so close that it couldn't be decided by counting votes alone, although strenuous and often inept attempts were made to interpret 'voter intention.' A ruling of the Supreme Court finally gave the presidency to Bush.

A few months later, tragedy struck. On September 11, 2001, terrorists hijacked four aircraft full of passengers. One plane was flown into the Pentagon in Washington, and two more into the twin towers of the World Trade Center in New York. The fourth plane came down on open ground in Pennsylvania. Close to three thousand innocent people were killed, and Bush declared a 'War on Terrorism.' Fear and panic struck America, perhaps for the first time. The economy shuttered.

More shareholder disasters came when huge corporations like Enron and Worldcom were shown to have connived with auditors to mislead the market over their true value, and Bush promised a 'new era of integrity.' Sadness struck at the American consciousness again on February 1, 2003, when during re-entry, the space shuttle *Columbia* disintegrated over Texas with the loss of all seven of the crew. The following month, without the support of the UN, American and British forces attacked Iraq.

These turbulent times have had a number of consequences, but the US always seems to bounce back. For instance, new architecture of major significance, like the revamped Museum of Modern Art in New York and Frank Gehry's Disney concert hall in Los Angeles, dazzle the eye and give a high-spirited glimpse of a gleaming future. Much like the country itself, as a matter of fact.

Historical Landmarks

1492 Explorer Christopher Columbus reaches America.

1620 Pilgrims aboard the *Mayflower* arrive at Cape Cod.

1773 In the 'Boston Tea Party,' tea crates are pitched over the sides of three ships in Boston Harbor to protest against taxes.

1776 On July 4, the Continental Congress in Philadelphia adopts the Declaration of Independence, penned by Thomas Jefferson.

1789 George Washington takes the first Presidential oath at New York's Federal Hall.

1804 Lewis and Clark set out on their 8,000-mile (13,000-km) expedition across America to the Pacific Coast.

1848 Gold is discovered at Sutter's Fort, California, bringing over 200,000 prospectors within the next three years.

1861 Confederates open fire on Fort Sumter, in the first shots of the Civil War.

1865 Civil War ends. Abraham Lincoln assassinated.

1929 Wall Street crashes, and with it comes the beginning of the Great Depression.

1941 Japan attacks Pearl Harbor, and the United States enters World War II.

1945 The first atomic bomb is detonated in New Mexico; bombs are dropped on Hiroshima and Nagasaki.

1955 Rev Martin Luther King, Jr leads the Montgomery (Alabama) bus boycott.

1963 President John F. Kennedy is assassinated in Dallas, Texas.

1969 *Apollo 11* takes two men to the surface of the moon.

1973–74 A world oil crisis plunges the US into economic crisis.

1989 An earthquake, 7.1 on the Richter scale, collapses a freeway and causes chaos in the San Francisco area.

1991 American-led forces liberate Kuwait in the First Gulf War.

2000 The presidential election is undecided by counting votes, so the Supreme Court gives presidency to George W. Bush.

2001 Hijackers fly passenger airliners into New York's World Trade Center and the Pentagon. A 'war on terrorism' is declared.

2004 New York City's Museum of Modern Art reopens after a major refit.

2005 A site search begins in Washington, DC to find the future location of the Smithsonian's National Museum of African American History and Culture.

WHERE TO GO

A trip to the United States is the gateway to a wealth of travel opportunity. Almost every imaginable kind of landscape, outdoor activity, and entertainment is available, many times over. From the natural wonders of the Grand Canyon, the Great Lakes and the mountains and coasts of the Pacific, to the megalopolises of New York, Las Vegas, and Miami, America has almost everything that the modern or the natural world can offer. You can enjoy whale-watching in Oregon, skiing in the Rockies, or café society in San Francisco. See unrivaled shows and gamble in Las Vegas, or watch world-class theater between shopping forays in Manhattan. America is the fourth largest country on earth, so there's a lot to see and do. Taking in even a representative sample involves at least

America's *Star Spangled Banner*, the national anthem, was written by composer Francis Scott Key in 1814.

a month and going to many destinations, although this is feasible. The most difficult question is 'where to start?'

If you are planning your first trip to the States, you may just want spend a couple of weeks in New York, Miami, San Francisco or one of the fabulous national parks. (A note about New York; the small island of Manhattan is untypical of the US in many ways. An important distinction for travelers is the use of the car. Almost indispensible anywhere else in the States, a car is just a burden in New York. Taxis, buses, and the subway are simple and efficient, and parking is a nightmare.)

For cross-country trips, Greyhound buses reach all over the continent. Trains are less practical, except along the East, Southern, or West coasts. Flying is often the best choice for long distances. On the 'shuttles' between New York and Washington or

Giant redwoods at Muir Woods National Monument

Boston, taking a plane is like taking a bus. But do try the bus or car if you can, to get a taste of the country's immensity and the American romance of the road.

From New York, the most convenient regions to include in a short stay are the Mid-Atlantic (Washington, DC, and Philadelphia) for the historically minded, and/or New England (Boston and the resorts in Massachusetts and Connecticut) for anyone who would like to mix history with relaxation. Or, there's Florida and the Gulf Coast in the South for those who want nothing but fun on the endless beaches, or at Walt Disney World Resort and other theme parks.

Another possibility for a two-week vacation is to combine New York with an excursion farther afield, either clear across the continent to California, or to one of the country's natural wonders such as the Grand Canyon or Yellowstone. New York, especially in summer, is an exhilarating but exhausting experience, so you'll need to pace yourself for the rest of the trip.

A Longer Stay

For a month-long stay, your itinerary might include New York-Boston-Washington, then directly to California, making your way back East via Yellowstone or the Grand Canyon, perhaps taking in San Antonio or Santa Fe for a taste of Southwestern America, followed by a distinctive big city like New Orleans, Chicago, or Las Vegas. Then finish up with a rest on a beach in Florida till your plane carries you home. If you want to see a lot of America in your four weeks, resist the temptation to start with California. You may be so seduced that you'll forget to look at the rest of the country.

The combinations are endless, but remember that Americans themselves like the good life to be both exciting and relaxed. If you want to survive your vacation, follow their example of enjoying both the big city *and* the parks or resorts. Even a town like Chicago has sandy beaches on the lake; New Orleans has its restful bayou country; New York has Long Island; Boston has Cape Cod; and there are beaches near much of Los Angeles.

NEW YORK CITY

Perhaps more than any other place on earth, New York is a city people feel they know before they arrive. Films and photographs have so stamped it into the popular consciousness that you believe that you're already familiar with the gigantic chasms of skyscrapers, the underworld steam puffing through the manhole covers, and the milling crowds of people.

Then, one day, you go. And it's more than you ever dreamed. Coming in to Manhattan from JFK airport, the city's skyscrapers loom higher, more impressive than in any movie. In the flesh, the crowds on Madison and Fifth avenues are a drama of color impossible to conceive of in the abstract. Right in there among the city's Irish, Italians, Chinese, Jews, Germans, Puerto Ricans, and African-Americans, not to forget the white Anglo-Saxon Protestants, you'll plunge into a unique travel adventure. Most other places have been discovered; New York is new every time.

Manhattan dazzles at night – here at Times Square

New York taxis are a good way to get around

While you can't know America without seeing New York, don't mistake it for the rest of the US. No other city has a more diverse population. Founded as New Amsterdam by the Dutch in 1626, the city numbered 1,500 inhabitants speaking 18 languages by 1644. Today more than 300 languages are spoken among the city's 8 million residents. While the terrorist attack of September 11, 2001 on the World Trade Center forever altered the face – and mindset – of New York, it did not diminish the enduring spirit of the 'greatest city in the world.'

The Island of Manhattan

This island, 13 miles (21km) long and 2 miles (3km) wide, encompasses almost everything you will want to see. The other four boroughs, Brooklyn, Queens, Staten Island, and The Bronx – all mostly residential, have their own special flavors, but for locals and tourists, Manhattan *is* New York.

Manhattan is a very easy place to find your way around. It divides simply into three basic parts: Uptown, Midtown, and Downtown (which, unlike other American cities, is the lower rather than the central part of town). Uptown is north of 59th Street, Midtown speaks for itself, and Downtown is the area south of 34th Street.

The backbone of the island is Fifth Avenue; all areas to the west of it as far as the Hudson are known as the West Side, while the East Side covers the area between Fifth Avenue and the East River. Fifth Avenue begins at Washington Square down in Greenwich Village.

There and in the Wall Street area, streets still have the names and irregular lines of the colonial era. Otherwise, all the roads intersect at right angles and the streets have numbers rather than names. The avenues (First to Twelfth) run north–south, and streets (1st to 220th) run east–west. Some avenues have names – York, Lexington, Madison, and Park. (Attempts to rename Sixth the 'Avenue of the Americas' have always seemed doomed.) Broadway, obeying no rules, runs more or less diagonally.

With the grid system of rectangular blocks, New Yorkers will pinpoint a place not by street number but by the nearest intersection of street and avenue; e.g., the Whitney Museum is at Madison and 75th, one block east and seven blocks south of the Metropolitan (Fifth and 82nd). This is the only form of location that a New York cabbie will accept for any location other than a major landmark.

Washington Square

Midtown

Your hotel may well be located in Midtown, so it's easy to cover the area on foot. One of New York's many distinctions is that it's a great city for walking in; sidewalks are wide and the crowds always interesting. At any rate, the center is the place to begin.

▶ **Rockefeller Center:** This soaring cluster of towers between Fifth and Sixth avenues, from 48th to 51st streets, is the undisputed magnetic core of New York City. Without any one of them being an architectural masterpiece, the ensemble of Indiana limestone buildings achieves a power and harmony that attract thousands of office workers, shoppers, street-vendors, and your better class of roustabout all day long.

The place breathes prosperity. John D. Rockefeller, Jr leased the site from Columbia University in 1928 to rescue it from the infamy of Prohibition speakeasy saloons. These quickly disappeared under the first skyscrapers of a booming business and communications center, linked by an underground pedestrian concourse, which includes over 200 stores and restaurants.

You immediately sense the cheerful genius of the place with the fountains and flower beds of the **Channel Gardens** that slope down from Fifth Avenue south of 50th Street to the sunken plaza. Akin to the English Channel, the gardens separate the Maison Française on the left and the British Empire Building on the right. At the end is **Rockefeller Plaza**, parasoled garden café

New York's Best Bridges

Water-laced New York has 65 bridges to hold it together, 14 of them connecting to Manhattan island. The 1,595-ft (486-m) Brooklyn Bridge created a sensation when it opened in 1883, but was plagued by misfortune from the start. Its engineer, John Roebling, died in the early phases of the project as a result of an accident. His son carried on and was paralysed in the course of the job. Nonetheless the bridge, with its wire webbing, is a beautiful success. It is illuminated at night for the best views. The 3,500-ft (1067-m) George Washington Bridge spans the Hudson between Manhattan and New Jersey. The Manhattan Bridge has spawned an artists' community called Down Under the Manhattan Bridge Overpass (DUMBO). Newest is the 4,260-ft (1,298-m) Verrazano-Narrows Bridge from Brooklyn to Staten Island, which opened in 1964.

Radio City Music Hall was built in the 1930s

in summer and ice-skating rink in winter. Watched over by a statue of Prometheus, the plaza is dominated by the center's tallest tower, the **GE Building**, home of NBC Television. The best way to see all that Rockefeller Center has to offer is to take one of the organized tours. The tours last one hour and fifteen minutes, and there's at least one departing every hour the center is open, which is every day except Thanksgiving and Christmas.

At one time, Rockefeller Center was supposed to be built around a new Metropolitan Opera House. Instead, they built **Radio City Music Hall** (tel: 212-621-6600), on the corner of Sixth Avenue and 50th Street. Radio City is one of the world's most marvellous movie theater-cum-variety-palaces – a brilliant 1930s pick-me-up for the Depression blues.

Try to see a show here, with the Rockettes, America's most famous troupe of dancing girls, kicking their legs to Radio City's own symphony orchestra and wonderful Wurlitzer organ, the world's biggest, as you might expect. At the very least, take one of the backstage tours organized seven days a week. The shimmering chandeliers and mirrors of the lobby would have impressed King Louis XIV. The auditorium, seating over 6,000, is ornamented with fantastic semicircular bands of light. It's hard to imagine that they nearly tore it down in the 1970s, but, as the *New York Times* said in support of the public outcry, 'If Radio City Music Hall really closes, it will be a little like closing New York.' Thankfully, they kept both open.

Fifth Avenue: This boulevard – at least the stretch between 34th Street and Central Park – is synonymous with luxury, to sample or to observe. If your budget won't stretch to a stay at the Plaza Hotel, you can bask in the understated opulence of the diamond-studded windows of Tiffany's jewelry store, or Cartier's, or Arpels & Van Cleef. Or stroll around the smart department stores like Saks Fifth Avenue, Bergdorf Goodman, or Henri Bendel or try the stylish high fashion of French and Italian boutiques like Gucci that take advantage of New York and New Yorkers' sophistication.

> New Yorkers tend to refer to Manhattan as 'the city,' even as they identify the other boroughs by name.
> For addresses, 'New York, New York' means Manhattan.

A Fifth Avenue gem is **Trump Tower** at 56th Street. Inside you will find the ultimate atrium, a cool, airy space six stories high, finished in rich rose-colored marble and gleaming brass. An appropriate collection of exclusive and expensive stores surrounds the courtyard.

Amid all this sometimes overripe elegance, turn off a moment at West 47th Street – '**Diamond Row**,' center of the diamond trade, where black-coated Hasidic Jews from Eastern Europe hurry back and forth with a glitter in their paper bags, under the benign protection of uniformed and plainclothes police.

The valiant effort of **St Patrick's Cathedral** (between 50th and 51st) to imitate Cologne's Gothic cathedral in Germany is a little lost today among the skyscrapers of Rockefeller Center and the Olympic Tower next door. But the 1879 building comes into its own on the occasion of the Irish-Catholic parade on

St Patrick's Day (March 17), when the Cardinal comes out to greet the marchers.

St Patrick's Cathedral

► **Times Square and Broadway:** The *New York Times* purports to publish 'All the News That's Fit to Print,' and the newspaper's Times Tower gave its name to that bizarre mixture of chic and sleaze – Times Square (on the north side of 42nd Street between Broadway and Seventh Avenue). Times Square in fact encompasses the area from 42nd to 47th Street, between Sixth and Eighth avenues. The heart of the theater district, it was also headquarters for the city's nastiest strip joints and sex shops. Excellent restaurants rubbed shoulders with the seamiest bars. Sleek limousines deposited ladies in evening dress, just down the street from prostitutes, drunks, and dope-dealers, all serenaded by street-entertainers similarly varying from the sophisticated talents of an out-of-work jazz musician to the crummy twanging of someone who stole a guitar.

But today, thanks to former mayor Rudolph Guiliani and committed community involvement, Times Square has undergone a major facelift. To the dismay of some and the relief of others, Disney is the anchor of this renovation, its presence towering over the corner of 42nd and Seventh. But now entire blocks have been redone. Old theaters that once showed horror and pornographic movies have been lovingly restored to their original beauty and purpose: legitimate theater. The headquarters of NASDAQ, Virgin Records and other shiny stores have replaced drugs and pornography, and the new neon lights expand the Broadway area known as 'the Great White Way.'

If the Times Square/Broadway atmosphere gets to be too much for you, relax in the snug armchairs of the lobby or the Blue Bar of the **Algonquin Hotel**, one of the greatest monuments of Manhattan's 1920s literary scene (44th Street, between Fifth and Sixth avenues).

42nd Street: Another haven of peace, as well as an architectural delight, is the **New York Public Library** (Fifth Avenue between 40th and 42nd; open Mon–Fri 9am–6pm). The building is a masterpiece of beaux-arts, a 1911 American reinterpretation of the French design school's neoclassical style at its gentlest and restrained best. Set back at the end of a wide stairway, the noble facade's three arches with coupled Corinthian columns around the entrance invite you in off the street for an hour's tranquility. In this most public of public libraries, relax with a book in the great reading room, admire the changing exhibitions in Gottesman Hall, or laze outside on the steps, where you are well protected by sculptor E.C. Potter's giant stone lions.

East on 42nd Street, at the south end of Park Avenue, **Grand Central Terminal**, terminus of the Vanderbilt railroad empire, is as much a legend as it is a building. Like the library, its beaux-arts pedigree is impeccable (although it took a US Supreme Court decision to save it from destruction). Over the great clock of the facade, the sculpture of the eagle among standing and reclining Roman deities apparently symbolizes America's special relationship with the gods. Completed in 1920, the station's 123 tracks built on two levels, 66 above and 57 below, move half a million people in and out of the city every day – mostly commuters from the suburbs. Watch them at rush hour in the vast barrel-vaulted main concourse, which has now been restored to its original splendor.

The **Met Life Building** over the station infuriated art critics at the time, but the neighborhood has some other impressive skyscrapers. A wonderful example of art deco can be seen in the stainless-steel swordfish pinnacle of the **Chrysler Building** (Lexington Avenue and 42nd Street). Of course, its glazed enamel, white-brick, and stainless steel silhouette is best seen glinting in the sunlight from a distance, but from the upper floors of nearby hotels you get a close-up of the weird gargoyles inspired by various radiator caps for Chrysler cars.

Be sure to take a look at the lobby inside the building, which, with its dark- and lightwood interior, is a near-perfect example of the stylish art deco form that swept the world in the 1920s and 30s.

The Chrysler Building

CitiGroup Center (Lexington Avenue between 53rd and 54th) brings an outstanding touch to the skyline with its dramatically sloping silver roof. At ground level, its urban consciousness is emphasized by a lively three-story 'market' of stores and restaurants around a skylit central courtyard. By the same architect, Hugh Stubbins, is free-standing, polygonal **St Peter's Lutheran Church** (42nd Street and Lexington Avenue). By no means overwhelmed by its skyscraper environment, the church has a lovely chapel decorated by sculptor Louise Nevelson.

Arguably the best of the sleek office blocks on Park Avenue is the **Seagram Building** (between 52nd and 53rd). Designed by Mies van der Rohe and Philip Johnson, the pure lines of this bronze-tinted glass skyscraper are considered the ultimate refinement of Mies' International Style. Inside is the Four Seasons restaurant and Picasso's stage-backdrop for *Le Tricorne*.

UN Secretariat building

The United Nations: (First Avenue, between 42nd and 48th; tours daily 9.30am–4.45pm). John D. Rockefeller, Jr, donated the 18-acre (7-hectare) site to persuade UN members to make their headquarters in New York. A team of international architects, led by the American Wallace K. Harrison and including the Swiss-French master, Le Corbusier, managed to put up buildings in the early 1950s with considerably more unity and harmony than are ever achieved inside by the diplomats. The Headquarters consist of four main buildings: the 39-floor Secretariat building; the General Assembly building (the lower block with the concave roof); the Conference Building; and the Dag Hammarskjöld Library, memorial to the late secretary-general, which was added in 1961. The complex is best seen as a whole from the East River on a boat ride around Manhattan.

At the information desk in the lobby (45th and First), you can get tickets for the General Assembly, when it's in session, and guided tours of the whole UN complex. Member states have donated parts of the complex – the three Council Rooms, for instance, being the gifts of Norway, Denmark, and Sweden, while Great Britain provided the Barbara Hepworth Sculpture in the plaza pool (the pool itself was a donation from American schoolchildren).

For a pleasant view of the skyscrapers along UN Plaza, buy a sandwich to eat in the garden, or have your lunch (passholders only; check about reservations at the lobby information desk) in the Delegates' Dining Room overlooking the East River. You can get reasonably priced crafts from all over the world at the gift shop. The post office here sells UN stamps only (not American) for letters and cards posted inside the complex.

Empire State Building: (corner of Fifth Avenue and 34th Street; open daily 9.30am–midnight). Everything about the Empire State Building is huge: 102 stories; 60,000 tons of steel; 3,500 miles (5,670km) of telephone wires and cables; 60 miles (97km) of pipes; the building occupies 1½ million cubic yards (1 million cubic meters) and King Kong had to climb 1,472ft (449m). Built in 1931, most of the building's office space was empty in the early Depression years and it paid its taxes with income from sightseers.

To get your ticket to the **Observation Deck**, go down first to the basement – arrows point the way. Next to the ticket office you'll find the Guinness World of Records Exhibit. The museum features life-size displays of world-record holders, videos, a data bank on sports, space, science, and music superlatives, as well as a huge sculpture of New York landmarks.

The Empire State Building

The elevator takes you to the 80th floor in less than a minute, then you catch the 'local' to the 86th. The outside platform offers a fantastic view, often of ships 40 miles (65km) out at sea, or in winter you may choose to remain inside the heated shelter for protection from the elements. There is also a third elevator that goes to an observation deck on the 102nd floor, but this is usually closed. The deck stands at the base of a 204-ft (62-m) high communications tower and antenna, from which TV and FM radio stations transmit programs to the metropolitan area. One of the most exciting aspects is the way the building changes color depending on the occasion: turning green for St Patrick's Day, or red, white and blue for the Fourth of July. For a complete list of lighting schedules and the occasions they represent, go to <www.esbnyc.com>.

Downstairs again on 34th Street, you're in a popular shopping area. Check out **Macy's**, or stroll over to 32nd and Seventh Avenue, where you'll see the entertainment and sports venue **Madison Square Garden**, 4 Pennsylvania Plaza, tel: (212) 465-6741, which claims to be the 'world's most famous arena.'

Downtown

Wall Street Area: Here at the southern end of Manhattan the skyscrapers close in on each other across narrow canyons to form ramparts for this almost awe-inspiring capital of capitalism known as Wall Street. Appropriately, the wall was conceived in 1653 as a protection for America's first great financial bargain – a wooden stockade to keep the Indians from invading the settlement on the island they had sold to the Dutch for the legendary price of $24 (60 guilders) 30 years earlier. Today, few addresses anywhere hold greater prestige.

The beating heart of the Financial District is the **New York Stock Exchange**, reverentially designed as a Roman temple. The action on the trading floor revolves around yelling traders, flashing computers and papers flying every which way – a roller coaster of buying and selling that keeps most American corporations in business. Unfortunately, the viewing platform to all this excitement is no longer open to the public.

From the exotic temple of

Wall Street reflections

the money lenders it's but a short step to **Trinity Church** (which dates from 1846) at the Broadway end of Wall Street. This, the first of America's Gothic Revival churches offers tired office workers – and weary sightseers – a few moment's rest and peace in the tranquil cemetery garden. Alexander Hamilton, the first Secretary of the Treasury, is buried here.

Fraunces Tavern

During the brief period that New York was the United States' first capital, the **Federal Hall** (corner of Wall and Nassau streets, demolished in 1812 and rebuilt in 1842) was the home of Congress and the place where George Washington took the oath as president on April 30, 1789. His bronze statue stands outside. The other landmark dating from the inception of the Republic is **Fraunces Tavern**, located at the corner of Pearl and Broad streets. It was here that Washington took leave of his officers at the end of the Revolutionary War, six years before his inauguration. The African-American tavern-owner, Samuel Fraunces, later became Washington's steward in the White House. The present building is an approximate reconstruction of the original.

World Trade Center Site: To the north of Trinity Church, the Twin Towers of the World Trade Center soared skyward until September 11, 2001. On an exceptionally clear and calm morning, two hijacked US passenger jets, under the control of terrorists, struck the towers in rapid succession and brought them down in the most heinous act of aggression in recent US history. The towers, which at 110 stories were the tallest buildings in the world at the time of their completion in 1973 and remained the tallest buildings in New York until their collapse, were totally destroyed in the attack. Also destroyed were the center's Mar-

Lady Liberty greets the masses

riott Hotel and two other near-by buildings. Two remaining structures in the World Trade Center complex were partially collapsed as a result of the unexpected attack.

Around 3,000 people, many of them policemen and firemen, perished in the catastrophy, amounting to the greatest single-day loss of human life in the US since the Battle of Antietam in the Civil War. A period of both public and private mourning ensued, culminating in a staged competition open to architects around the world to come up with an appropriate replacement.

The building selected was Daniel Libeskind's Freedom Tower. When completed, it will rise 1,776 ft (541 meters) into the air, and will once again be the tallest in the world. Meanwhile, mourners and shocked visitors who witnessed the attacks on TV congregate at the site, which for the forseeable future is a noisy, disorienting construction site. To reflect on the tragedy in more peaceful surroundings, go to nearby **St Paul's Chapel**, which has a permanent display, or to the *Icon of Hope* in Battery Park, a global sphere that was pulled from the wreckage of the towers.

> **Statue of Liberty:** (15-minute ferry ride from Battery Park; tel: 212-269-5755 for prices and schedules). It is difficult to imagine a more eloquent symbol than the message this 'Lady' of the Statue of Liberty offered those desperate refugees sailing to the New World at the end of the 19th century. Today, few Americans or foreigners, however cynical, can remain totally blasé about this monument, rising 305ft (93m) from its pedestal base to the tip of the torch. The statue, built by French

sculptor Auguste Bartholdi and structural engineer Gustave Eiffel, was a gift from the people of France, presented on July 4, 1884 and erected here in 1886. The statue's full name is 'Liberty Illuminating the World,' a French idea linking the French and American revolutions. The $250,000 it cost was jointly and privately funded, with the French paying for the statue and the Americans for the pedestal. Visitors climb the steps to the pedestal, where a glass ceiling provides a view into the intricate interior structure. Timed passes eliminate extremely long waits.

West of Liberty Island is **Ellis Island**, where 12 million of those 'huddled masses' passed through immigration checks between 1892 and 1924. The medically suspect were marked with chalk on their lapels – H for heart, K for hernia, Sc for scalp, X for mental defects. Today, the 'island of tears' has been declared a national monument; the old immigration station restored and turned into the **American Museum of Immigration**, which tells the often-wretched stories of the millions who passed through here.

If you don't want to join the crowds on Liberty Island, but want a cooling boat ride as well as a marvelous view of Manhattan,

---

Invitation to Hope

Symbolically, the Statue of Liberty was the first sight of the new world for many millions of immigrants arriving by boat over the last two centuries.

The famous inscription on the pedestal of the Statue of Liberty was written by Emma Lazarus, a New York poet, in response to the Russian pogroms of the 1880s which drove so many Jews to cross the Atlantic.

Her lines have since taken on a universal significance, and shone as a beacon of hope for all the world's oppressed:

'Give me your tired, your poor,
Your huddled masses yearning to breathe free,
The wretched refuse of your teeming shore.
Send these, the homeless, tempest-tossed, to me:
I lift my lamp beside the golden door.'

take the **Staten Island Ferry** (also from Battery Park, tel: 212-269-5755). It's the best bargain ride in town: passengers travel for free. For a superior view, stand forward on the second deck.

Lower East Side: The area from Canal Street north to Houston is where the immigrants headed first. Most stayed just long enough to learn English and then headed Uptown or beyond the Hudson River. Chinese, Jews, and Italians chose to settle here a little longer in their own enclaves. The Chinese are still here in strength, and although the area is becoming increasingly trendy – full of boutiques and hot music clubs – the colors, sounds, and smells of the other communities also linger on vividly enough for you to capture, in an easy afternoon's stroll, the old flavor.

If you take the East Side subway to **Chinatown**, you won't go wrong: the Canal Street station has signs in both Roman and Chinese characters. The telephone booths have pagoda roofs, stores sell jade jewelry, grocers display snow peas and winter melon, and countless restaurants vie for attention with their Cantonese, Shanghainese, and Szechwan specialties.

Well over 100,000 Chinese live in Chinatown, a loosely defined area centered around Canal Street, Mott Street, and Chatham Square. The earliest arrivals came to the country during the California Gold Rush in the 19th century; most of the immigrants today come directly from Hong Kong. To learn about the history and sites of the area, visit the **Museum of Chinese in the Americas** (70 Mulberry Street).

Many Chinese from the rest of New York (and even from other parts of the state) come here on weekends to do their grocery shopping and to enjoy a meal out. Supermarkets sell the finest China teas, and pretty porcelain to drink it from. Take a look at the **Buddhist Temple** (64 Mott Street), where you can purchase your fortune for a small sum.

South of Mott Street, at 55 St James Place, is the city's oldest 'monument,' the Shearith Israel cemetery, founded in 1683 by Portuguese Sephardic Jews from Brazil. But Manhattan's historic **Jewish Quarter**, settled principally by Eastern European

Ashkenazi Jews, is on the northeast side of Chinatown, around the old Hester Street market. Walk along Delancey and Orchard streets and you'll see only a shadow of its hey-day, but you can sense how hectic it once was.

Peaceful and tranquil on the Sabbath from Friday evening to Saturday night, the place springs back to life on Sundays, and where the clothing stores and delicatessens ring with accents from the Jewish villages of Polish Galicia and Ukraine. For a snack, try a

San Gennaro Festival, Little Italy

pastrami (seasoned smoked beef) sandwich and a cup of lemon tea in one of the excellent kosher restaurants.

Even tinier than its name suggests, **Little Italy** is centered on Mulberry Street a few blocks to the northwest – and shares its southern part with Chinatown. The Italian section is now princi-pally a gastronomic hub, with expensive as well as moderately priced restaurants and espresso bars, high-quality caterers, and, scattered among them, souvenir shops and the occasional gro-cery store specializing in scrumptious home-made and imported Italian delicacies. The street is at its liveliest during the 10-day Feast of San Gennaro in September, and be sure to come with a good appetite.

Greenwich Village and SoHo: The village was once New York's artistic center, home of such illustrious writers as Mark Twain, Edith Wharton, John Dos Passos, and O. Henry and painters like Edward Hopper, Ben Shahn, and Franz Kline. In the 1950s, villagers swayed to the jazz of Miles Davis and Bill Evans at the Village Vanguard; in the 1960s to hear the first jokes of Woody Allen at the Bitter End Café. The venerable and lively **Village Vanguard** (178 Seventh Avenue South, tel: 212-255-4037) still sports a fine jazz roster.

At night the jazz cellars are as aromatic as ever, and a few remaining coffee houses serve good espresso over which you can read your weekly *Village Voice* newspaper. A bygone charm can still be found in **MacDougal Alley** and **Washington Mews**, while the hottest trends and coolest restaurants in town can be sampled in the cobbled streets and former butcher shops of the **Meatpacking District**, the northwestern part of the Village.

Henry James lived for a few months on **Washington Square**, the title of one of his novels and heart of the New York University campus. His grandmother lived in one of the Greek Revival houses along the north side (No. 19), a very elegant dwelling. Look up and enjoy this stretch of Fifth Avenue from **Washington Arch**, the work of the architect Stanford White, commissioned in 1889 to mark the centenary of George Washington's inauguration as president.

> **Washington Square, at the south end of Fifth Avenue, is where locals congregate during the hot summer months.**

In the 1970s the area south of West Houston Street, **SoHo** (short for **So**uth of **Ho**uston), followed the pattern of Greenwich Village. Artists who couldn't afford the rents after the village's commercialization moved south to the abandoned lofts and warehouse floors of this industrial district. The most successful artists were able to install kitchens, bathrooms, and comfortable interiors. Others made do with bare walls and floors for the sake of the ample space and light. With the success of the avant-garde galleries on West Broadway, especially No. 420, where Pop Art's Andy Warhol, Robert Rauschenberg, and Roy Lichtenstein displayed their works, rents soared. The interior decorators and restaurateurs took over from the artists, many of whom moved out, first heading southwest to **TriBeCa** (**Tri**angle **Be**low **Ca**nal), later to Chelsea and, finally, to the borough of Queens.

Upper West Side, Central Park, and Uptown

The Upper West Side – that is, west of Central Park – defies any label to its neighborhoods other than 'mixed.' Intellectuals and artists live side by side with the shopkeepers and bus drivers of all backgrounds. Street life is active and harmonious. Central Park has been called 'the lungs of New York,' a place where city-dwellers can relax and breathe. Uptown includes the lively and historic area of Harlem.

Lincoln Center: (West 62nd to 66th, between Columbus and Amsterdam, tel: 212-875-5030; one-hour guided tours of Lincoln Center start at the concourse level of the 'Met'). With most of the prestigious fine-arts museums located on the affluent Upper East Side, the Lincoln Center for the Performing Arts provided a good balance and a perfect fillip for the revival of the neighborhood in the 1960s. Since Daddy had to shelve his plan to put the Metropolitan Opera in Rockefeller Center, John D. Rockefeller III led

The Lincoln Center for the Performing Arts

the drive to find it another home, along with the New York Philharmonic, the New York City Ballet, and the Juilliard School of Music. The center replaced a Puerto Rican neighborhood of the kind immortalized by Leonard Bernstein's musical comedy *West Side Story* – Bernstein moved on, too, after a stint with the Philharmonic.

As you go up the steps to the plaza on Columbus Avenue – especially at night with the central fountain bathed in ethereal light – you may find the effect a little too self-consciously 'prestigious.' New Yorkers do take their arts seriously. The undoubtedly important buildings around the plaza are overwhelmingly monumental, starting on the left with the modern classicism of Philip Johnson's **New York State Theater**, home of the New York City Ballet and New York City Opera. Men can't help adjusting their ties and women straightening their dresses when entering the opulent lobby with its gilded-chain drapery and gold-velvet ceiling.

New Yorkers are fond of their abbreviations. SoHo means South of Houston and TriBeCa is a contraction of the 'Triangle below Canal' Street. A newer addition to the vocabulary is Brooklyn's DUMBO, or Down Under Manhattan Bridge Overpass.

At the back of the plaza, Wallace K. Harrison's grand design for the **Metropolitan Opera House**, with its tall glass facade arched in travertine marble and red-carpeted lobby with dazzling Austrian crystal chandeliers, makes it almost an impudence to call it the 'Met.' You can see the immense paintings by Marc Chagall from the plaza.

Originally completed in 1962, **Avery Fisher Hall** had to have its hall reconstructed several times over the next 14 years before achieving today's excellent acoustics and admired architectural simplicity. At the back of a handsome reflecting pool with sculpture by Henry Moore is the **Vivian Beaumont Theater**, originally intended as the base for a New York repertory company. Designed by Eero Saarinen, it houses a large round auditorium with a versatile movable stage at plaza level and the small Mitzi Newhouse Theater below.

A bridge across 65th Street connects Lincoln Center to the **Juilliard School**, a world-famous music conservatory. On the first floor, in its Alice Tully Hall, you can hear chamber music ensembles and afternoon concerts by the best Juilliard students.

Central Park: A vast green breathing space in the center of Manhattan (½ mile/1km wide and 2½ miles/4km long), Central Park is a sports field, playground, and picnic spot for tens of thousands of city-dwellers. In the 1840s, the poet William Cullen Bryant realized that New York needed more parks for its rapidly expanding population. He launched a campaign to persuade the city to buy the land – then wasteland beyond the city limits, inhabited by squatters. Landscape gardeners Frederick Law Olmsted and Calvert Vaux were called on to design the park, which took 3,000 workers 16 years to complete. Conceived in the English style, the park doesn't really look manmade – the Lake, the 'forests,' the paths, and the meadows seem to have been there since time immemorial. The 75,000 trees, flourishing despite the shortage of soil and abundance of rocks, are home to countless squirrels and birds. By day it's perfectly safe to walk in the park, but be wary of those around you. Avoid the park at night, unless you're going with a group to the summer theater or music events.

Central Park

Starting from the southeast corner of the park, skirt the Pond to the small, modern **zoo**. Then stop in at the **Dairy**, the Central Park Visitors' Center, for a calendar of park events. From here, head up the wide, tree-lined Mall to the ornamented **Bethesda Fountain and Terrace**. In summer, you can hire a rowboat at the Loeb boathouse – to your right – for a trip on the pretty lake stretching out below the terrace. To the east, at the oval **Conservatory Water**, permit holders sail their miniature boats next to statues of Hans Christian Andersen and Alice in Wonderland. On a hill level with the Metropolitan Museum of Art stands **Cleopatra's Needle**, a 3,000-year-old obelisk that was a gift from Egypt in the late 19th century.

A more recent addition to Central Park, **Strawberry Fields**, (at Central Park West between West 71st and 74th streets) is Yoko Ono's horticultural memorial to her husband, John Lennon, who was murdered in 1980 just across the street, in front of the Dakota apartment house (1 West 72nd Street). The 1½-mile (2.5km) path around the **Reservoir** is popular with joggers. Sports are played in the park every day, but most of all on Sundays in the summer. There are miles of bicycle and jogging paths, which are turned into cross-country ski runs in winter, along with tennis courts, an ice-skating rink, and playgrounds for children.

Free open-air concerts and operas are presented on the **Great Lawn** during the summer months, and in **Belvedere Castle** there are exhibits and special events. The **Delacorte Theater**, south of 81st Street on the west side of the park, has a good Shakespeare in the Park Festival (free; line up ahead of time for tickets).

Harlem: Harlem, the cradle of African-American culture, has undergone a second renaissance in recent years, marked by the arrival of former president Bill Clinton, who established an office here in 2001. Harlem's main thoroughfares bustle with shoppers choosing among well-known mall retailers, local merchants, and street vendors, some of them offering exotic wares. A drive through Harlem is included in many sightseeing tours of Manhattan, and a number of local agencies offer jazz and gospel tours. Important museums include the **Schomburg Center for Research in Black Culture** (515 Malcolm X Boulevard) and the **Studio Museum** (144 West 125th Street). For tour bookings, contact NYC & Company (tel: 212-484-1222; <www.nycvisit.com>).

Harlem stretches from the northern reaches of Central Park to 178th Street. In the 1950s, it was the home of a million African-Americans from the southern states and the Caribbean. Today barely a quarter of a million remain. Optimists attribute this exodus to the housing programs and improvements in living standards. Pessimists say that dilapidation just drove people out to ghettos such as the South Bronx.

One of Harlem's many churches

Founded by Dutch settlers, Harlem remained a village separate from the rest of Manhattan until the end of the 19th century, when middle-class Americans moved north away from the new immigrants of the Lower East Side. You can still make out the genteel facades of some of their houses. African-Americans started moving in around 1920, the beginning of the Jazz Age. Leaving the cottonfields of the South, New York was the 'Promised Land.' Duke Ellington and Cab Calloway played the Cotton Club and the Savoy, drawing crowds of white people Uptown, where, during Prohibition, alcohol was easier to obtain. Now emerging from years in the crime-ridden doldrums, renewal is spreading. There's jazz at the **Lenox Lounge** (288 Lenox Avenue at 125th Street) and **Showmans** (375 125th Street), soul food at **Sylvia's** (328 Malcolm X Boulevard), and variety entertainment at the resurrected **Apollo Theater** (253 West 125th Street), where Amateur Night again reigns on Wednesday evenings.

Around Edgecombe Avenue the architecture becomes quite impressive. Here live wealthy African-Americans who stayed put during Harlem's decline and are now enjoying its resurgence. One of New York's last remnants of the colonial Georgian architecture is the **Morris-Jumel Mansion** (Edgecombe at West 160th Street, tel: 212-923-8008; open Wed–Sun 10am–4pm), a stately house set in a picturesque garden. Built in 1765 and used as a headquarters by George Washington at the beginning of the Revolutionary War, it was bought in 1810 by a French wine-merchant, Stephen Jumel. Jumel's widow, Eliza, a remarkable woman who claimed to have slept with both George Washington and Napoleon, married her second husband, Aaron Burr (third vice-president of the US), here. Now it is a museum of American decorative arts from the 18th and 19th centuries.

The east side of Harlem is a mainly Puerto Rican community also known as **Spanish Harlem**. Visit **El Museo del Barrio** (Fifth Avenue at 104th Street, tel: 212-831-7272; open Wed–Sun 11am–5pm), a museum devoted to the art and culture of Latin America. In summer months, take in the atmosphere of colorful **La Marqueta**, a market on Park Avenue.

Metropolitan Museum of Art

Museums in New York City

With its 120 museums, New York performs a unique service to world civilization as a cultural bridge between the Old and New worlds. You could spend a lifetime in them.

Metropolitan Museum of Art: (Fifth Avenue at 82nd Street, tel: 212-535-7710; open Sun-Thur 9.30am–5.30pm, Fri–Sat 9.30am–9pm, closed Mon). Indisputably one of the world's great museums, the Metropolitan consists of nearly 250 rooms with over 4,500 paintings and drawings, one million prints, 4,000 musical instruments, and countless pieces of furniture and sculpture. Only a quarter of the collection is on display at any one time. Especially interesting are the American Wing, a glorious celebration of the architecture, decorative arts, and fine arts of the United States; the Lehman collection of early Italian and French Impressionist painting; the primitive art in the Michael C. Rockefeller wing; the sections devoted to European painting from the 15th to the 20th centuries; the Islamic art section and the extensive Egyptian department.

Museum of Modern Art: (West 53rd Street between Fifth and Sixth avenues, tel: 212-708 9400; open Wed–Mon 10.30am–5.30pm, until 8pm Fri, closed Tues.) MoMA to habitués, this fantastic museum boosted by the Rockefeller family has more than 100,000 works of art from 1880 to the present. An ambitious and highly successful 'refit' in 2004 virtually doubled the exhibition space, the better to see MoMA's breathtaking collection, including Vincent Van Gogh's *The Starry Night* and Pablo Picasso's *Les Demoiselles d'Avignon*.

Guggenheim Museum: (Fifth Avenue and 89th Street, tel: 212-423 3500; Sat–Wed 10am–5.45pm, Fri 10am–8pm, closed Thur). Designed by Frank Lloyd Wright, the museum's architecture is as important as its contents: late 19th- and 20th-century collections as well as works by Paul Klee, Kandinsky, and Chagall. The annex offers fine Van Gogh, Gauguin, and Modigliani paintings and a wonderful group of Picassos.

Whitney Museum of American Art: (Madison Avenue and 75th Street, tel: 212-570-3676; open: Wed–Thur and Sat–Sun

11am–6pm, Fri 1–9pm). Drawing on the great vigor of American 20th-century art, the museum has marvelously lit, imaginative, and adventurous exhibitions.

Frick Collection: (70th Street and Fifth Avenue, tel. 212-628-0700; Tues–Thur and Sat 10am–6pm, Sun 1–6pm). Industrialist Henry Clay Frick's classical European paintings, furnishings, and other treasures are presented in the opulent and intimate setting of his own home.

American Museum of Natural History: (Central Park West at 79th Street, tel: 212-769-5100; open daily 10am–5.45pm). Renowned for its remarkable collection of dinosaur skeletons, it also has a planetarium, along with striking zoological dioramas and important anthropological exhibitions.

Cooper-Hewitt Museum: (Fifth Avenue and 91st Street, tel: 212-849-8400; open Tues–Thur 10am–5pm, Fri 10am–9pm, Sat 10am–6pm, Sun noon–6pm). America's largest collection of decorative art from the 15th to the 20th centuries.

Museum of Jewish Heritage – A Living Memorial to the Holocaust: (18 First Place, Battery Park City, tel: 1-646-437-4200; open Sun–Tues and Thur 10am–5pm, Wed 10am–8pm, Fri and eve of Jewish holidays 10am–3pm). Dedicated to 20th-century Jewish art and recollections of Holocaust survivors.

Jewish Museum: (Fifth Avenue at 92nd Street). Jewish ceremonial objects, archaeological remains from Israel, and excellent avant-garde art shows.

Museum of the American Indian: (1 Bowling Green, State and Whitehall streets). A collection of Native American art and artifacts displayed in the historic Custom House.

Museum of the City of New York: (Fifth Avenue and 104th Street). Important for the town's exciting history. Great old toys.

Pierpont Morgan Library: (Madison Avenue and 36th Street). Rare books, Old Master paintings, Florentine sculpture, etc., amassed by the American industrialist J. Pierpont Morgan.

Intrepid Sea-Air-Space Museum: (Pier 86, 46th Street and 12th Avenue). Centered on the converted World War II aircraft carrier *Intrepid*, with planes on the deck and displays below.

Excursions from New York City

Atlantic City (NEW JERSEY): (*From New York, Lincoln Tunnel and south via the Garden State Parkway*) Atlantic City has made its way into most American homes via the street names in the American version of Monopoly. But from around 1900 until the World War II, it was a major northeast entertainment center, featuring the likes of Benny Goodman, Duke Ellington and, later, Frank Sinatra. It went into serious decline beginning in the 1950s, until gambling brought it back to life in the 1970s. The casinos are now its main attraction, although the quaint charm has not entirely disappeared from the painted facades of the stores along the 6-mile (10-km) long **Boardwalk**, still laden with amusements, tacky temptations and bargains. The sea breeze is always refreshing, especially accompanying a mouthful of Atlantic City's famous salt-water taffy.

The thundering Niagara Falls

Niagara Falls (NEW YORK STATE): The most remarkable attraction in New York State is Niagara Falls, where nature still manages to triumph over tawdry commercialism. No amount of pushy pedlars or 'honeymoon motels' can diminish the awesome spectacle of that mass of white water plunging nearly 200ft (60m) on its way from Lake Erie down toward Lake Ontario.

It's worth looking at the falls from more than one perspective. Make your first vantage point Goat Island, a nice mini-tram ride from Prospect Point. The island divides the

waters of the Niagara River into the eastern **American Falls** –
182ft (55m) high, 1,076ft (323m) wide – and the western
Horseshoe (Canadian) Falls – 176ft (54m) high and 2,100ft
(640m) wide – with a smaller cascade known as Bridal Veil off
to the side. On Goat Island you can choose between a helicopter
tour over the whole falls area or an elevator (sometimes closed)
down to where the white water crashes into the lower river bed.

There you can walk behind the wall of cascading water and
experience the cataract's overpowering roar. Tour operators provide protective clothing, but nothing is totally waterproof
against Niagara. Cable-cars take you high above the rapids;
three boats, all named *Maid of the Mist*, give you a safe view
from the river. More adventurous, but not unsafe, is the Jetboat
trip through the rapids at the base of the falls. There are numerous observation towers, the best being on the Canadian side
(foreign visitors should bring their passports). The viewpoints of
the Skylon and Minolta towers are respectively 770ft (235m)
and 665ft (203m) above the falls.

At night the Horseshoe Falls gleam in multicolored illumina-
tions with 4,000 million units of candlepower generated by the
falls themselves. The United States and Canada have collabor-
ated to exploit Niagara's tremendous power resources –
2,190,000 kilowatts on the American side and 1,775,000 kilowatts on the Canadian side. Four miles (6.5km) north on Route
104, is the interesting **Niagara Power Project** showing how this
energy is harnessed. A geological museum in Prospect Park de-
scribes how rock erosion will completely flatten out the falls in the
next 30,000 to 40,000 years.

You might like to make a side trip to **Buffalo**, a charming city
with a lively cultural life. The Albright-Knox Art Gallery (1285
Elmwood Avenue) has some fine examples of American and
European art of the 18th, 19th, and 20th centuries. The gallery is
set in lovely **Delaware Park**, landscaped by Frederick Law
Olmsted, which includes a zoo with some Buffalo buffalo. The
first-rate Buffalo Philharmonic Orchestra gives concerts at the
Kleinhans Music Hall.

NEW ENGLAND

From north to south, New England comprises six states – Maine, New Hampshire, Vermont, Massachusetts, Rhode Island, and Connecticut, with Massachusetts' Boston as the undisputed capital. Their combined area would scarcely cover just one state in the West, but their historical significance in the American republic's exciting beginnings and their present role in political and cultural life are essential to the United States.

Beyond the historic fascination of New England, there's a terrific adventure to be had along the rugged coastline and

Autumn at Harvard

little fishing ports from the Canadian border down to Boston. Farther south lie the glorious sandy beaches of Cape Cod, while inland are the rolling hills of the Massachusetts Berkshires, the dramatic White Mountains of New Hampshire, and the lovely woods that cover four-fifths of the New England landscape.

Crisp, fragrant spring and drowsy, hazy summer are delightful times in New England, but the trees claim a special short season to themselves in the place where the expression 'Indian summer' came into being. After the first cool spell in autumn, there's a sudden new burst of sunshine, when warm days and cool evenings combine to create a spectacular explosion of color in the leaves. The gold of the poplars and birches, the scarlet of the oaks, dogwoods, and maples, and the magical copper-orange of the mountain ash and hickories are a draw for visitors from far and wide. This natural spectacle has become

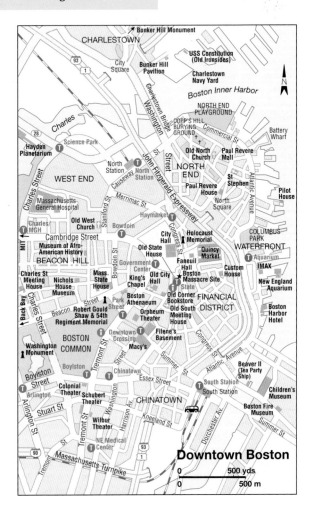

Downtown Boston

0   500 yds
0   500 m

such a popular draw that you can telephone state and local tourist offices to get up-to-the-minute information on where to see the best displays, which usually peak around mid-October. This is also a great time for country fairs, communal flea markets, garage sales *(see page 210)*, and pay-for-what-you-pick apples and pears in the orchards.

Boston *(MASSACHUSETTS)*

This Massachusetts city encompasses the essence of America's origins and the blossoming of its 20th century. It's a bustling place of 600,000 people inside the narrow city limits, but nearly 4 million if you include all the townships of metropolitan Boston. Those small towns capture America's beginnings, while the big city, packing 70 colleges into the metropolitan area at the center of the huge 'brains industry' – New England's greatest resource – is working on the country's future.

With the student population, Boston houses the Anglo-Saxon descendants of the original settlers, the very proper 'Brahmins' in the elegant neighborhood of Beacon Hill. They now play a distinguished second fiddle to the Irish who spread through the town since fleeing the 1845 potato famine, first as laborers, then as 'lace-curtain' bourgeois, until reaching the heady heights of the Fitzgeralds moving into City Hall and the Kennedys into the White House. The Italians make up an equally lively community, based in the town's North End. The African-American community, with a proud past in Boston as the first freed slaves, is largely concentrated in Roxbury and Dorchester.

Boston is a good town to walk around. The narrow streets of the most interesting sections make driving difficult, and parking is almost impossible. So park your car outside the city and take the 'T' subway (underground) to the city's heart, **Boston Common**. Between Tremont, Boylston, and Beacon streets is the green nucleus of the 50 acres (20 hectares) that the Massachusetts Bay Company bought from a beleaguered hermit, the Reverend William Blackstone, in 1634. Already here when the 900 Puritans arrived, he sold out when he couldn't take any more of their officious manners. As if to make his point for him, they established on the green, as well as the usual grazing for livestock, a pillory and stocks, whipping post, sinners' cage, and gallows. The first victim of the pillory was its carpenter, punished for charging too much for his work. In the old Puritan days, it was the one public place where Bostonians were permitted to smoke tobacco. Today the Common is popular with students and residents alike playing baseball and touch football.

Immediately west of the Common is the **Public Garden**, reclaimed in the 19th century from the marshes south of the Charles River. The neat little flower beds made up the country's first botanical garden. The artificial pond in the center provides gentle rides on board its **swan boats** in summer, and ice skating in winter. The **Visitors Information Center** is on the Tremont Street side of the Common, a good place for maps and brochures and orientation for the 1½-mile (2.5-km) **Freedom Trail** around the city's principal historical sights. The route is marked by a painted red line or by red bricks set in the sidewalk.

Tranquil-looking, white-steepled **Park Street Church** was built in 1809. At one time this was called Brimstone Corner – as

Revere's Ride

Thanks to Henry Wadsworth Longfellow's exciting if frequently misleading poem, Paul Revere got all the glory for the ride to alert the fighting men of Lexington and Concord. In fact he was, luckily, not alone. The British caught up with him soon after he reached Lexington; his co-riders William Dawes and Sam Prescott carried the news on to Concord. All the same, Revere's versatility and devotion to the American cause won him a prominent place in history.

He also rode with important Massachusetts legislative resolutions to the First Continental Congress in Philadelphia.

An accomplished silversmith, he made the noble Liberty Bowl, on show at Boston's Museum of Fine Arts. And he was one of the 'Mohawks' at the Boston Tea Party.

the church served as a gun-powder mill during the war of 1812. Just as explosive were the first anti-slavery speeches that were delivered from its pulpit in 1829 by abolitionist William Lloyd Garrison. In the church's **Old Granary Burial Ground** are buried Paul Revere, Sam Adams, and John Hancock, signatories to the Declaration of Independence. Children may be interested in the tombstone of Mary Goose, said to be the original Mother Goose of nursery rhyme fame.

Park Street Church

The **Old South Meeting House** (Washington and Milk streets), originally a Puritan church (1729) and now a museum of the Revolution, is best remembered as the place where Sam Adams planned the dastardly Tea Party. The British used it as a riding school during their occupation of Boston, burning the pews and pulpits for firewood, but the rest of the original woodwork is intact.

Farther along Washington Street, the **Old State House** (1712) was the British Governor's Residence, and it is still graced by the lion and unicorn of the royal coat of arms (copies of the originals that were burned on Independence Day, 1776). A monument marks the spot where Crispus Attucks, an African-American man and the first martyr of the Revolution, was shot.

Faneuil Hall (rhymes with 'panel'), 75 State Street, has earned its name as the 'cradle of liberty' as the site of two centuries of speeches by politicians from Sam Adams to John F. Kennedy. Susan B. Anthony spoke out here against the slavery both of African-Americans and of women.

The 1798 State House, architect Charles Bulfinch's masterpiece

From Faneuil Hall, make your way via Union and Marshall streets under the Fitzgerald Expressway to **North End**, now the colorful center of the Italian community – fresh pasta shops, aromatic grocery stores, and pizza parlors amid charming old houses topped by attractive roof gardens.

Resume the Freedom Trail here on North Square at the wooden-frame **Paul Revere House** (tel: 617-513-2338, open daily) the oldest house in Boston, built soon after the disastrous city fire of 1676. The Revolutionary hero moved here in 1770, five years before he set off to make his historic ride, famously alerting New Englanders to the emergency that, 'the British are coming.'

The intrepid horseman's statue can be seen north of his house on Paul Revere Mall, with the fine **Old North Church** (1723) behind him. It was in the church tower, designed in the style of Christopher Wren and restored after being toppled in a 1954 hurricane, that two lanterns were hung to signal to Revere that the British were marching out. An interesting feature is the unusually tall pew boxes. They were built for parishioners to huddle in against the fierce Boston winter winds.

The Freedom Trail continues across Charlestown Bridge to the site of the Revolutionary War's first pitched battle at **Bunker Hill**, which was attended by George Washington, a general in the American army. But if that's enough history for the time being, you can make your way back to Faneuil Hall.

To the east of it is **Faneuil Hall Marketplace**, a lively haven tucked among the administrative buildings of Government Center and the newer skyscraper office blocks. This center of boutiques, galleries, restaurants, and cafés is one of the country's most successful pieces of urban restoration, and was a model used throughout America.

The central domed building is Quincy Market, specializing in gourmet foods. South Market offers art galleries, jewelry, and gift stores, while North Market has fashion boutiques.

Recapture the city's old serenity on **Beacon Hill**, the handsome neighborhood sandwiched between Government Center and the Common. Here among the cedars and chestnuts and gas lanterns of **Mount Vernon Street** and Louisburg Square, you can admire the restrained glories of Boston's finest residential architecture. Boston-born Charles Bulfinch was one of the principal designers of the US Capitol in Washington, DC, as well as America's first native-born professional architect. He developed his signature Federal-style houses here in the city, and the fine but simple red-brick facades are the very essence of New England dignity.

Louisburg Square, with its residents' fenced-off garden in the center and the three-story curved, bow-fronted houses, will remind some of Georgian London. Others are modeled with the popular Doric-columned porches of Greek Revival.

This can be seen in its most monumental form in Bulfinch's **Massachusetts State House**, off Beacon Street, which was completed in 1798, after the cornerstone was laid by Paul Revere and Sam Adams 1785. It was this building, with its its impressive doric portico and gilded dome, that earned Bulfinch the Washington commissions, which earned him his place in architectural history.

Back Bay, west of the Public Garden, was a bay at the rear of Boston's 19th-century city center until landfill turned it into a residential neighborhood with a Victorian character for the city's newly rich merchants. Now it is enlivened by chic boutiques and art galleries, and is dominated by the towering Hancock and Prudential skyscrapers.

Both buildings offer excellent observation decks on their top floors, although the architecturally more satisfying of the two is I.M. Pei's elegant **John Hancock Tower** on Trinity Place at St James Avenue, sheathed in reflective glass. There's a grand view from the 60th floor (half a minute in the elevator) over Cambridge and Charlestown all the way to the New Hampshire mountains. Be sure to check that these observation decks are open before you set out.

Museums in Boston

Museum of Fine Arts: (465 Huntington Avenue, tel: 617-267-9300; open Mon–Tues 10am–4.45pm, Wed–Fri 10am–9.45pm, Sat–Sun 10am–4.45pm). One of the best collections in the country. American, European, and Asian works are well laid out. Don't miss I.M. Pei's west wing.

Isabella Stewart Gardner Museum: (280 The Fenway, tel: 617-566-1401). Wonderful European collection in a building that recalls a Venetian *palazzo*.

Children's Museum: (Museum Wharf, 300 Congress Street, tel: 617-426-8855). Children can blow giant bubbles, visit a Japanese house, and climb through a multilevel maze. There's an indoor play area and a 'supermarket' for smaller children.

The Tea Party Ship

Museum of Science: (Science Park). Innovative exhibits in paleontology, physiology, light and perception, a full-immersion virtual fish tank, a real fish hatchery, planetarium, IMAX theater, and the interactive Cahners ComputerPlace.

Beaver II, **Tea Party Ship:** (Congress Street Bridge on Harbor Walk, Pier 1, Pratt Street). A replica of one of the British ships raided in the protests against the duties on tea.

Cambridge *(MASSACHUSETTS)*

There is more to see in Cambridge (separated from Boston by the Charles River) than the prestigious college, **Harvard**. Founded by the Massachusetts Bay Colony as America's first university in 1636, it is named for a young churchman, John Harvard, who bequeathed it £780, half his worldly wealth, and his library of 320 books. Now the college has an endowment of $6.2 billion and about 100 libraries with over 10 million volumes. In 1965, Harvard merged with Radcliffe College for women (founded in 1894), and the combined institutions now number over 36,000 students. They have the use of 17 university departments, nine faculties, more than 50 laboratories, two astronomical stations, and nine excellent museums.

At the western end of Massachusetts Avenue, **Harvard Square** is a bustling introduction to the town, with cafés, restaurants, bookstores, and the 'Coop' (short for 'cooperative' but pronounced like a chicken coop), reputedly the country's biggest university store. For orientation around the campus, start at the **Information Center** in the rather daunting modern block of **Holyoke Center**, just south of the square. The campus clusters mainly around **Harvard Yard**. Unlike university architecture elsewhere in the country, Harvard avoids the 'Collegiate Gothic' of spired towers, unimaginatively recalling Oxford and Cambridge in England. Harvard went for the more traditional New England style of red brick, still seen in **Massachusetts Hall** (1720) and **Harvard Hall** (1766), along with the clapboard of **Wadsworth House** (1727), formerly the home of college presidents. The one concession to Gothic Revival is **Memorial Hall** (1878), a Victorian structure commemorating Harvard's fallen in the Civil War.

There are lovely 18th-century houses along Brattle Street, west of Harvard Square, known as Tory Row after their Loyalist owners. At No. 105 is the **Longfellow National Historical Site**, poet Henry Wadsworth Longfellow's home from 1837 to 1882. Built in 1759, it was General Washington's headquarters for the siege of Boston. Most noteworthy of the campus's modern buildings is the **Carpenter Center for the Visual Arts** (24

Quincy Street), the only building in North America by influential architect Le Corbusier.

The **Geological and Mineralogical Museum** exhibits minerals, gems, and meteorites, and a dramatic model of a Hawaiian volcano. At the **Museum of Comparative Zoology**, look for the world's oldest egg (65 million years old) and the 25,000-year-old Harvard Mastodon, found in New Jersey in 1844. The **Botanical Museum** is also known as the Glass Flower Museum for over 3,000 plant specimens modeled life-size in glass at the Dresden workshop of Leopold and Rudolf Blaschka.

If you return to Boston via Harvard Bridge, stop off at the **Massachusetts Institute of Technology** along Massachusetts Avenue. With its solid research in the natural and social sciences, in engineering, architecture, and urban planning, MIT has created for itself perhaps the most prestigious academic initials in the world. The MIT **Museum** joins imagination and technology in exhibits of kinetic light sculptures, holography, artificial intelligence, and stroboscopy, while the Hart Nautical Gallery celebrates innovation in the exploration and maintenance of our oceans. The campus rewards the visitor with striking buildings designed by Finnish architect Eero Saarinen: the Kresge Auditorium and the MIT **Chapel** on Amhurst Street.

Excursions from Boston

➤ **Lexington** (*MASSACHUSETTS*): (*From Boston, take Interstate 93 to the Woburn exit west*). Almost engulfed by the expanding web of metropolitan Boston, Lexington still has the classical elements of a small New England country town. There's an immaculate **village green**, with a tavern on one side and a church on the other.

This was the town into which Paul Revere rode on the evening of April 18, 1775, to warn colonial leaders John Hancock and Sam Adams that the British were coming. Their target: American arms and ammunition in nearby Concord. The tavern is Buckman Tavern, which served as rallying point for 77 Minutemen, rustic militia so called because they had to be ready at a minute's notice. At one end of the village green is a statue of the Minutemen's leader, Captain Parker. At the other, inscribed on a boulder of the **Revolutionary Monument**, are the captain's heroic words: 'Stand your ground; don't fire unless fired upon; but if they mean to have a war, let it begin here.'

It did, at 5am on April 19, when the first of 700 British soldiers arrived. The British ordered the militia to disperse, but a shot rang out and the British opened fire. In the skirmish, eight Minutemen died, and the wounded were taken to **Buckman Tavern**, which you can see today restored to its 18th-century glory. For those who spare a thought for the poor British – they did suffer 272 casualties

Minute Man Monument on Lexington Green

before they got back to Boston from this fateful sortie – there are also guided tours of the 17th-century **Munroe Tavern**, which doubled as the British field hospital and headquarters.

Salem *(MASSACHUSETTS): (North on Route 1 and 1A from Boston):* The name Salem, from the Hebrew word 'Shalom,' meaning peace, is somewhat ironic considering the town's violent history. Salem is known primarily as the site of the USA's most infamous witchcraft trials; it's also famed for its more glorious maritime past.

In 1692, a slave's tales of sorcery had a strong effect on two young Puritan girls. Their gossip led to mass hysteria, witch hunts, and the hanging of 19 'witches.' For the best retelling of this gory story, visit the multimedia exhibit at the **Salem Witch**

Provincetown Bay at the northern end of Cape Cod

Museum on Washington Square. The 17th-century **Witch House** on Essex Street, home of witch-trial judge Jonathan Corwin, is restored and worth a visit.

With the witchcraft era behind it, Salem soon became a prosperous seaport and home to America's first millionaires. Down at Derby Wharf, **Salem Maritime National Historic Site** tells the story of Salem's great seafaring days; the old **Customs House** across the street can also be visited. Ship owners made a fortune out of the China trade, and many of their spoils – from Burma, India, Indonesia, China, Japan, and Korea – are now on display at the **Peabody Essex Museum**, the oldest continuously operating museum in America. The same museum also protects several splendid houses on Essex Street.

At No. 128 is the **Gardner-Pingree House** (1804), by Salem architect Samuel McIntire – an outstanding example of the Federal style. Note the simple elegance of the rose-brick facade topped by a white-wood balustrade and the wonderful woodwork of the interior. The Peirce-Nichols house (1782) at 80 Federal Street is also by McIntire.

Salem is also known as the birthplace and home of 19th-century novelist Nathaniel Hawthorne, who worked at the Customs House. His **House of the Seven Gables**, at 54 Turner Street on the waterfront, is the oldest living history museum in the US.

Besides being a historic treasure, Salem, with its green common, traffic-free center, and restored waterfront (visit the stores and restaurants on pretty Pickering Wharf) is a lovely place to wander.

Cape Cod (*MASSACHUSETTS*) (*Interstate 93 out of Boston, Route 3 to the Cape*): The beaches, sand dunes, and marshlands of Cape Cod's east coast are both invigorating and relaxing. It was a surprise to no one when, in 1961, President Kennedy made the coast a protected area – the **Cape Cod National Seashore**. It had, after all, been his family's holiday home for years.

The easiest way to reach the National Seashore is via the high-speed ferry to **Provincetown**, at the northern tip of Cape Cod. Provincetown itself is a busy tourist center with plenty of boutiques and galleries and renowned for its 'anything goes' attitude (it's one of the the East Coast's main gay meccas).

But here on the outer elbow facing the Atlantic Ocean you can listen to the pounding surf and stroll the awesome beaches that are backed by huge dunes. Access to the dunes is strictly controlled and limited to boardwalks at some points. The National Seashore has two Information Centers: the Salt Pond Center, near Eastham on Route 6, and Province Lands Visitor Center just outside Provincetown. Both provide detailed information on the terrain, natural life, and activities. At Province Lands, take the opportunity to climb on to the roof for a panoramic view of the dunes, Another great view can be had from a hillock northwest of Pilgrim Lake in the **Pilgrim Heights** area. The Pilgrim Spring Trail takes you to a spot where, according to local legend, in 1620 the people of the *Mayflower* drank their first American fresh water.

At the southernmost tip of Cape Cod, Woods Hole ferries go across to Martha's Vineyard (45-minute crossing) and Nantucket

(3 hours) – two island resorts that are popular with discerning New Englanders and New Yorkers. There are no wild grapes growing on **Martha's Vineyard** anymore, but the local population drinks plenty of wine. You can get around the island by shuttle bus or rent a bicycle or moped. The beaches are excellent, Katama on the south shore being especially prized by surfers. For a lovely view, go west of Katama up onto the **Gay Head Cliffs**, which consist of layers of colored clay – red, orange, gray, blue, and ocher. The local Indians turn this clay into pottery. Equally brightly colored are the charming gingerbread cottages of **Oak Bluffs**, while the grander houses of **Edgartown** are made of sparkling white clapboard.

Nantucket Island is just right for the family. The beaches on the north side of the island are washed by the warm waters of the Gulf Stream, and offer easy swimming. Hardier swimmers go to Cisco and Surfside for the big breakers of the south shore. Nantucket town, beautifully preserved on the cobbled **Main Street**, has a proud whaling history (ending abruptly in the second half of the 19th century when Pennsylvania oil replaced whale blubber). At the **Whaling Museum** (Broad Street) is all the sailor's paraphernalia of the whaling industry. If you're taken by the impressive exhibition of scrimshaw, you may want to buy some in the waterfront stores on **Straight Wharf**, at the end of Main Street.

Gay Head Lighthouse, Martha's Vineyard

Plymouth (*MASSACHUSETTS*): On your way from Boston to Cape Cod, stop off on Route 3 to pay homage to the site of New England's founding. A boulder on the edge of the harbor is said to be the legendary **Plymouth Rock** onto which the first *Mayflower*

Pilgrim stepped in 1620. Today, the boulder is protected by monumental granite pillars. Few countries in the western world celebrate the historic sites of their beginnings with more reverence. North of the rock, at State Pier, is *Mayflower II,* a replica that sailed from England in 1957. Just south of the town is **Plimoth Plantation**, a living museum of the Pilgrims' first village of 1627: thatch-roofed, clapboard cottages with period English furniture, barns, and stables. Costumed actors playing historical individuals charm you with their 17th-century world view and dialect. Nearby is a replica of a period Wampanoag encampment.

The Berkshires (*MASSACHUSETTS*): (*Interstate 90 from Boston or Interstate 87 from New York*): The rolling foothills at the western end of the state at the border with New York state, loosely called the Berkshires, offer wonderful opportunities in the summer to combine music, dance, and theater with hiking and fishing. The Berkshires are the place for watching the fall foliage, and there's skiing in winter. Dotted among the hills are the grand 19th-century estates that provided summer homes for wealthy New Yorkers and Bostonians and are now resort hotels.

> **Illustrator Norman Rockwell's home and studio, as well as a museum of his work, can be seen in Stockridge, Massachusetts.**

Since 1934, the **Tanglewood** estate (just outside Lenox) has been home to the summer Berkshire Music Festival. Its Music Shed, designed by Finnish architect Eero Saarinen, seats 6,000 people. A nice way to enjoy the concerts in good weather is to come for a picnic a couple of hours early and listen to the music (at a much lower price) from the lawn. The Chamber Music Hall holds other concerts.

The Berkshire Theater Festival is at the Playhouse in **Stockbridge** (south of Tanglewood on Route 7). The town itself is well worth a visit. It was established in 1734 by four white families who had the explicit goal of converting the local Mohican Indians to Christianity. Reverend John Sergeant's **Mission House** (1739), Route 102, austere and even gloomy by modern standards but considered plush in its day, is now a museum of that pious era.

The **Old Corner House**, appropriately on Main Street, was the home of painter/illustrator Norman Rockwell, beloved observer of American Main Street life for the covers of the *Saturday Evening Post* magazine. The **Norman Rockwell Museum** (Route 183, Stockbridge) documents the evolution of his work, from the details of small-town Americana in the Depression years to the more recent struggles of racial integration and urban violence, and covers other well-known illustrators (Rockwell Kent, Maxfield Parrish) as well.

Farther south, around Great Barrington, there is some first-class fishing and hiking country along the Housatonic Valley.

MID-ATLANTIC REGION

Seven years after the end of the War of Independence, the northern and southern states finally agreed on a site for the nation's permanent capital – right between the two regions, on land ceded by the states of Maryland and Virginia. A visit to Washington, DC, and a swing through the surrounding states will give you an opportunity to compare the businesslike North with the more leisurely South. Is Philadelphia still the 'handsome city' that Dickens described? Is Virginia as stately as the old plantation-days image? What about Washington itself? In frustration, President John F. Kennedy said the capital had the charm of a northern city and the efficiency of a southern town.

Washington, DC

Washington, DC could only be the capital of a great republic. Monuments and ministries are everywhere. But the architecture leans more to the temples of ancient Greece and Rome than to the palaces and cathedrals of the European monarchies, and the government buildings are in a green and pleasant setting. The 69 sq. miles (179 s.q km) of the city (an area conterminous with the District of Columbia) include 33 parks, relics of the old Maryland estates and plantations.

Over 3 million people live in Greater Metropolitan Washington and the suburbs in Virginia and Maryland; the city itself numbers just under 600,000 residents (572,000 in the 2000 census, down from 606,900 in 1990), more than half of them African-American.

The Capitol and North Fountain, Washington, DC

The government center of civil servants, congressional representatives, senators, diplomats, and journalists leads a life largely separate from the concerns of the metropolis, which is beset, like any other large American town, with slums and crime. For visitors too, this underbelly remains mostly out of sight, as they stick to the downtown federal district and its residential neighborhoods to the northwest.

When you see the attractive houses and diplomatic missions around Massachusetts Avenue, and the university district of Georgetown, you may find it hard to believe that for a long time Washington was just marshland on the banks of the Potomac River. To lay out the new capital, George Washington called on the Paris-born engineer Pierre Charles L'Enfant, the man who had remodeled Federal Hall in New York for the presidential inauguration. But the valiant Frenchman, a major with the US Army during the Revolutionary War, produced a radical plan for the central federal district inspired by Rome and Versailles, which proved a little too ambitious for the young Republic's treasury. After a quarrel with the bureaucracy, who called him

'L'Enfant terrible,' he was fired and died in misery, although his designs for the city were later more fully realized.

Apart from the White House – only half finished when John Adams moved in in 1800 – the place looked much like a ramshackle frontier town for most of the 19th century, in part because it was sacked and burned by the British in 1814. The Capitol took 70 years to complete, and the streets weren't paved or properly lit till after the Civil War. It was only in the 20th century that Washington assumed the shape of L'Enfant's grand conception – perhaps it took that long to find the money – and the architect was reburied, with honors, at Arlington National Cemetery.

Considering all there is to be seen, the area covering Washington's sights is surprisingly compact. It's practically all in a rectangle extending from Union Station and the Library of Congress, in the east, to Watergate and the Lincoln Memorial near the Potomac River, in the west. Georgetown is just northwest of this rectangle and Arlington National Cemetery is on the west bank of the Potomac. Nearly all the monuments and museums are free of charge.

When you don't feel like walking – Washington can be very hot and sticky in high summer – an agreeable alternative is the system of open-sided Tourmobile shuttle trolleys. They follow a route past the main monuments, museums, and government buildings, stopping at convenient points around the Capitol, the Mall, and the White House. Guides provide cheerful commentaries as you ride. The advantage is that you can get on and off as often as you like with one all-day ticket (bought on the trolley when you first board). The Tourmobile also undertakes excursions to Arlington and Mount Vernon *(see pages 94 and 100)*.

Public transportation in Washington includes an efficient municipal bus service together with a pleasant and extensive underground Metrorail network. Taxis are plentiful, charging – not exorbitantly – by the zones into which the town is divided (see the map in the cab) rather than by meter. Zone One covers most of the main sights. Keep your car for out-of-town excursions, because legal parking Downtown is expensive and illegal parking is disastrous. The police do not hesitate to tow vehicles away to one of 20 compounds without letting you know, even by telephone, which one.

The White House *(1600 Pennsylvania Avenue, NW):* Although the White House used to be open to the public, because of anti-terrorism precautions, there are now only limited tours with advance reservations; these are generally available only to American citizens who can arrange them through their congressional representative. You can still get a reasonable sense of the White House and its history if you stop by the **Visitor Center** at 15th and E streets in the Department of Commerce building (daily 7.30am– 4pm; closed Jan 1, Thanksgiving Day, Dec 25; tel: 202-208 1631 or <www.whitehouse.gov>, or for information regarding special events tel: 202-456 7041). The Park Rangers who staff the center are helpful and there are several exhibits, a 30-minute film entitled *Within These Walls*, and a gift shop.

The White House

Even when the White House was open to the public, the tour was only 20 minutes long, and there were never any costumed docents on duty to offer commentary or answer questions – a strange arrangement, considering the building's rich history.

The White House was designed in 1792 by Irish-born architect James Hoban in the English Palladian style popular with the landed gentry. In the competition for a $500 gold medal, Hoban beat an anonymous entry by Thomas Jefferson.

Happy to reside there himself in 1801, Jefferson declared the building 'big enough for two emperors, one Pope and the grand Lama.' That opinion didn't discourage him from promptly adding a terrace pavilion on either side while Benjamin Latrobe was putting on the porticos. This set the pattern for nearly all Jefferson's successors – though without the benefit of his architectural training – of remodeling or redecorating their temporary home.

Visitors lucky enough to go inside the White House follow roughly the following tour: on the ground floor is a corridor that looks out onto the Jacqueline Kennedy Garden, then the Vermeil Room (with its collection of gilded silver serving pieces) and the Library. Upstairs is the State Floor, containing the five rooms that are most familiar to the public from books and TV.

The **East Room**, where presidential press conferences are held, is used for concerts, balls, and receptions – weddings for the president's children, funeral services for presidents who die

---

Toasting the White House

It wasn't always the president who 'redesigned' the White House. In 1814, the dastardly British Admiral George Cockburn led an assault on Washington and the White House in retaliation for American pillage in Canada *(see page 22)*. While President James Madison had gone off to join the militia, wife Dolley stayed behind to take care of the valuables, getting out just before the British arrived and set fire to the place. A providential thunderstorm put out the fire but not before the White House turned decidedly black.

in office, notably Lincoln, Franklin D. Roosevelt, and Kennedy. The White House's first First Lady, Abigail Adams, used it as a drying room for her laundry. The famous 1796 Gilbert Stuart portrait of George Washington was saved from the 1814 fire by Dolley Madison, wife of President James Madison.

First ladies often hold tea parties in the elegant **Green Room** under a wonderful 1790 cut-glass chandelier given by the British to President Herbert Hoover. Jefferson liked to take his dinner here, showing off to baffled Americans the latest gourmet ideas he'd imported from Europe, such as macaroni, waffles, and ice cream.

The oval **Blue Room** is decorated in French Empire style appropriate to the state dinners held here. Outside the windows is 'Truman's Balcony' where the president from Missouri used to take the air. The **Red Room** with its red-satin walls has some impressive gilded and marble tables. Its opulence contrasts with the restrained decor of the **State Dining Room** at the western end of this first floor (underneath the presidential living quarters). Dominated by a portrait of Abraham Lincoln, it's done in fine 18th-century English style, walnut Queen Anne chairs against oak paneling with Corinthian pilasters.

The Mall and Potomac Park: The Mall – an expanse of greenery and water from the Capitol to the Lincoln Memorial, crossing the axis between the White House and the Tidal Basin at the Washington Monument – is undoubtedly one of the country's great urban vistas. It is almost always full of people strolling, relaxing, flying kites, and playing ball, surrounded by monuments and museums. It's a posthumous triumph for planner Pierre Charles L'Enfant, whose dream it had been to achieve this harmonious interplay of the built environment with nature.

If the Statue of Liberty represents America to the world, then the **Washington Monument** symbolizes the nation for Americans themselves. This 555-ft (169-m) white marble obelisk seems to state, with the noble simplicity of George Washington himself, the people's loftiest aspirations. Construction of the

Abraham Lincoln, immortalized in the Lincoln Memorial

monument began in 1848 but dragged on for 36 years because of lack of funds and the interruption of the Civil War. There's an elevator to the top for a great view.

West of the obelisk, wander along the tree-lined, 2,000-ft (610-m) long reflecting pool to the **Lincoln Memorial** (1922). This Greek-temple–like structure, a white rectangular box surrounded by 36 Doric columns, houses the 19-ft (6-m), seated statue of a pensive Abraham Lincoln by Daniel Chester French. There is a wonderful effect at daybreak when the majestic sculpture is first lit by the rising sun.

On the left of the entrance is a plaque with Lincoln's speech after the (Civil War) Battle of Gettysburg, when he paid tribute to those who had died for a 'nation conceived in liberty and dedicated to the proposition that all men are created equal.'

Pause at the **Vietnam Veterans Memorial** nearby. This simple monument to the Vietnam war dead carries the names of 58,000 soldiers killed or missing in action. The more conventional statuary group was added later at the request of many of those who served. From here you can make a detour across

Potomac Park and around the Tidal Basin to the **Jefferson Memorial** (1943), inspired by the Pantheon in Rome.

As you look at the bronze statue of this architect, philosopher, and most elegant of statesmen, you might recall the eloquent words of President Kennedy. At a dinner given in the Blue Room of the White House for Nobel Prize winners, he said, 'I think this is the most extraordinary collection of talent, of human knowledge, that has ever been gathered together at the White House – with the possible exception of when Thomas Jefferson dined alone.'

The Mall goes past one of the world's most impressive concentrations of museums and galleries *(see pages 98–100)*. South of the brooding statue of Civil War General Ulysses S. Grant, stop off at the **Botanic Garden**. A three-year renovation added new environmental exhibits to this extensive international collection.

Capitol Hill: The most powerful government in the western world deserves a setting like the Capitol. This massive edifice imposes its will under a huge white dome that joins the Senate in the north wing to the House of Representatives in the south. The place exudes power.

William Thornton's original design in 1793 was a low-domed affair. When Benjamin Latrobe expanded the design after the British burning of 1814, the homespun Congressmen complimented him only on the corncobs and tobacco leaves with which he rather whimsically decorated the Corinthian columns of their chamber. Charles Bulfinch came from Boston to put on a bigger and better dome, but by 1850 Congress, sensing that America was going places, wanted it even bigger. So Thomas Walter, with nothing less than St Peter's in Rome for his model, hoisted an iron dome up on a grandiose columned 'drum' and that, with Thomas Crawford's statue *Freedom* topping it off in 1863, is the way it stands today.

The Capitol is entered from the east side, starting at the **Rotunda** (there are normally 45-minute guided tours). The vast ceiling is decorated by a fresco painted by Constantino Brumidi in 1865, *The Apotheosis of George Washington*, showing him glorified by the deities of Liberty, Victory, and Fame and 13 ladies representing the 13 original states. Below is a 300-ft (91-m) frieze devoted to American historical events from Columbus through Cornwallis's surrender at Yorktown to the flight of the Wright brothers' aircraft in 1903.

In **Statuary Hall** and the corridors leading off the Rotunda, you'll see what is widely regarded as one of the most delightfully horrendous sculpture collections in America. It's the result of an act of cultural democracy by which each of the 50 states was invited to exhibit its most famous citizens, portrayed by the state's own sculptors.

Outside, the Capitol's grounds cover 131 acres (53 hectares) of charming parkland designed by the 19th-century landscape architect Frederick Law Olmsted, well-known for his parks in Boston, New York, Chicago, and California.

The **Library of Congress** (1st Street and Independence Avenue), packed with millions of books, maps, manuscripts, periodicals, photographs, recordings, and rare instruments, is one of the great institutions of Capitol Hill. For the visitor, the permanent exhibition of documents includes the 1455 Gutenberg Bible, one of only three in the world to have survived in perfect condition. See also the poignant Civil War photographs of Matthew Brady, first of the great American photo-journalists, in the Prints and Photographs section.

> **The Library of Congress attempts to keep two copies of every book in the English language in stock.**

Behind the Library of Congress, the **Folger Library** (201 East Capitol Street) offers in its Tudor interior the largest collection of Shakespeareana outside Britain, including a nicely reproduced Elizabethan theater. Next door, the awe-inspiring **Supreme Court**, built in 1935, is the last of Washington's government buildings in the Graeco-Roman style. For anyone interested in the workings of the American legal system, court hearings can be attended between October and June.

The Supreme Court, built in 1935

North and South of the Mall: The scene of Abraham Lincoln's assassination, **Ford's Theater** (511 10th Street, between E and F streets, tel: 202-347-4833; open daily, but for matineé performances only on Thur noon–3.30pm, and Sun 2–5pm) has been preserved as a National Historic Site, meticulously restored to how it looked on April 14, 1865. Since 1968, it has been operating again as a theater, complete with presidential box. The basement is now a museum of Lincoln's life. It preserves the clothes he wore to the play, the Derringer pistol that killed him, and the diary of assassin John Wilkes Booth, Shakespearean actor and embittered supporter of the lost southern cause. Across the street, at No. 516, is **Petersen House**, where the dying president was taken – the streets too badly paved for a safe trip back to the White House. You'll see the bleak little bedroom where the 6-ft 4-inch (2-m) Lincoln had to be laid diagonally across the bed.

The FBI **Headquarters** in the J. Edgar Hoover Building (Pennsylvania Avenue between 9th and 10th streets) is one of the most popular destinations in Washington, and reservations are recommended (tel: 202-324-3447; open Mon–Fri 8.45–2.30pm) for its hair-raising tour. An introductory film explains the workings of the Bureau and documents its historic cases, from the gang-busting days of the 1930s to the investigations of civil rights activities in the 1960s and the threats to national security of the present day. Then you'll see the gangsters' guns and Hoover's Ten Most Wanted Men. The laboratory displays the FBI's latest gadgetry for uncovering criminals. At the tour's climax, your special agent guide gives a demonstration of marksmanship, in which all agents are required to be proficient. His or her .38 calibre revolver and a submachine-gun are fired into a paper man-sized target – offered as a souvenir to someone's lucky child.

For an enlightening experience, visit the **National Archives** (Constitution Avenue between 7th and 9th streets), where you can see the original documents of the Declaration of Independence, the Federal Constitution, and the Bill of Rights, all handwritten on parchment. Some have faded badly but are now surrounded by light-filtering glass, with helium protection against decay.

South of the Mall, at 14th and C streets, is the **Bureau of Engraving and Printing** (tel: 202-874-2330; tours May–Aug, otherwise 9–2pm; valid photo ID required) where you can see the printing of US paper money and postage stamps, from a one-cent stamp to a $500 million Treasury Note (no photographs llowed). Follow the journey of the blank white sheets made of cotton and linen through inking and cutting to the delicious stacking of crisp dollar bills at the other end. Each bill takes 15 days to produce and will usually disintegrate after 18 months of normal use. You can buy shredded money for a souvenir.

Arlington *(VIRGINIA):* Running north behind the Lincoln Parkway between Rock Creek Parkway and the river is a delightful half-mile walk along the green riverbank. On weekends you can see polo, field hockey, jousting on horseback, and even canoes paddling by. You'll pass the **Kennedy Center for the Performing Arts**, (2700 F Street), less admired for its clumsy architecture than for its cultural activities in a capital that previously neglected the performing arts. The center comprises two theaters, an opera house, a concert hall, and the American Film Institute's excellent 'cinémathèque.' Farther north is the wavy complex of the Watergate apartments, where in 1972 dirty tricks were perpetrated, resulting in the downfall of President Richard Nixon, who was forced to resign rather than face impreachment.

Beautifully situated on a hillside on the opposite bank of the Potomac is **Arlington House** (also known as the the Robert E. Lee Memorial). This sober Greek-Revival mansion fronted by eight Doric columns was built by George Washington's adopted grandson, George Washington P. Custis, in 1812. It was later the home of General Robert E. Lee until he left to lead the Confederate armies in 1861. Immediately in front of the house is the grave of the architect Pierre Charles L'Enfant, commanding the best view across the river of the capital he so lovingly planned. A granite slab is engraved with his original plan. It's a chance to compare the plan with the result.

Arlington National Cemetery

During the Civil War, Union troops confiscated Lee's house, and part of its surrounding plantation was used as a burial ground for the war dead. Out of this grew **Arlington National Cemetery**, in which only American soldiers who have seen active duty can be buried.

Pride of place goes to the **Tomb of the Unknowns** (soldiers of the two World Wars and the Korean War), guarded by a solitary infantryman ceremoniously changed every half hour in summer, every hour in winter. In its own small park, the **John F. Kennedy Grave** is a square of simple paving which is set around an eternal flame. Jacqueline Kennedy Onassis is buried in the same plot, and John's brother Robert Kennedy is buried nearby.

The Marine Corps War Memorial, better known as the **Iwo Jima Statue**, is located outside the north entrance to the cemetery. Standing 78ft (23m) high, this is the world's tallest bronze statue, featuring five marines and a sailor hoisting the American flag (a real one is raised daily by Washington-based marines) on Mt Suribachi during the battle for the Japanese Pacific island base of Iwo Jima on February 23, 1945. It took three more weeks to capture the island, with the loss of over 5,000 men – but Japanese losses were four times higher.

Attractive, affluent Georgetown

Georgetown: Within the District of Columbia directly northwest of the downtown federal district, Georgetown is the home of Washington's elite in government, the diplomatic corps, university establishment, and better-paid journalists. It's also the liveliest part of town, with bright, pleasant stores, art galleries, cafés, and restaurants, centered on M Street and

Wisconsin Avenue. It's one of the only parts of Washington with a cheerful street life after dark – the perfect antidote to any overdose of museums and officialdom.

Georgetown was laid out in 1751 and was already established as a major tobacco market when the town of Washington was still being planned. Georgetown exported tobacco along the Potomac and imported luxury goods such as silks, wines, tinware, tea, and powder for the wigs of its highstepping gentry. A couple of houses survive from that era, but most of its better residential architecture is Georgian and Federal style from the first half of the 19th century, with a little Victorian 'heavy pastry' from after the Civil War. Its narrow, shaded streets are a fine change from the broad avenues of governmental Washington.

The oldest house in town is the 1766 **Old Stone House**, at 3051 M Street, now a museum of colonial life. Another noteworthy Georgian edifice is **Dumbarton House** (2715 Q Street), remodeled by Benjamin Latrobe in 1805. It's now a museum of federal period furniture, silver, and china. Its public programs include lectures on 18th and 19th century furniture styles as well as concerts.

Dumbarton Oaks (3101 R Street), an imposing mansion built in 1801, was the site of the 1944 conference at which the US, Britain, the Soviet Union, and China drew up the blueprint for the United Nations. The 16 acres (6.5 hectares) of grounds are a delightful mixture of formal terraces and pools with more informal English-style landscaping on a lower level. The gardens include (at 1703 32nd Street entrance) the mushroomdomed Museum of Pre-Columbian and Byzantine Art, designed by Philip Johnson.

A charming surprise at the southern edge of Georgetown is the remnant of the **Chesapeake & Ohio Canal** (the 'C&O'). Serving as an artery for coal-hauling from 1828 to 1924, it now welcomes loafers, hikers, cyclists, canoeists, and fishermen – and in winter, as in a Brueghel painting, skaters. Canal Square (1054 31st Street) is an old canalside warehouse converted into a shopping center.

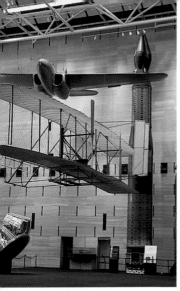

The National Air and Space Museum

Museums in Washington

National Gallery of Art: (Constitution Avenue between 4th and 6th streets, tel: 202-737-4215): The West Building, a classical, columned temple of art, is devoted to European and American painting and sculpture, with exhibits from the Middle Ages to the present day. Its strength is in Italian art, but the French, Dutch, German, Flemish, Spanish, British, and American schools are splendidly represented as well. I.M. Pei's design of the East Building is a breathtaking combination of geometric forms – soaring triangles segmented into piercingly acute angles. The effect is even more exhilarating inside, where the museum's collection of contemporary art is on display.

The Smithsonian Institution: (tel: 202-357-2700). Not one museum but a huge umbrella collection grouping many museums – 14 in Washington, a couple in New York and branches in other cities. The museums have a combined inventory of 75 million artistic and scientific items, only 1 percent of which is ever on display. All museums are free.

National Air and Space Museum: (7th Street and Independance Avenue). The whole history of the adventure of flying, whether it be the Wright brother's first lift across a meadow in North Carolina in 1903 or Neil Armstrong's journey just 66 years later from Cape Canaveral to the moon and back, is packed into these 23 galleries.

National Museum of Natural History: (10th Street and Constitution Avenue). Everything from an 80-ft (24-m) long Diplodocus to the creepy, crawly Insect Zoo. The building also houses the Museum of Man, including displays of Inuit and Native-American artifacts.

National Museum of American History: (Madison Drive, 12th to 14th streets). Depicts US life from different periods and social strata, with definitive exhibits on the history of electric lights and motors.

National Museum of the American Indian: (4th Street and Independence Avenue). A collection showcasing thousands of masterworks, including carvings and masks from the Northwest; quilled hides and feather bonnets from the Plains; pottery from the Southwest; 18th-century materials from the Great Lakes, and beautiful Navajo weavings.

Hirshhorn Museum: (Independence Avenue between 7th and 9th streets). Modern art displayed in this drum-shaped building, highlighted by a sculpture garden featuring Rodin's *Burghers of Calais* and pieces by Moore, Picasso, and David Smith. The painting collection includes examples of Cubism, Social Realism, Op, Pop, and Minimalism.

Freer Gallery of Art: (Jefferson at 12th Street). A major Asian collection and a smaller American one.

Art and Industries Building: (Jefferson at 9th Street). In high Victorian style, this building houses an important collection of Americana and other exhibits from the 1876 Philadelphia Centennial Exposition.

Arthur M. Sackler Gallery: (1050 Independence Avenue SW). Buddhist sculpture, ancient Iranian metalwork, and about a thousand works of art from China, Southeast Asia, and the ancient Near East are housed in these beautiful subterranean galleries.

National Portrait Gallery: (8th and F streets). All the presidents and great ladies are here, including Pocahontas, Eleanor Roosevelt, and Gertrude Stein; also a major center of historical photography.

Museum of American Art: (8th and G streets). Fine examples from colonial times via Winslow Homer, Cassatt, and Whistler to O'Keeffe and de Kooning.

Renwick Gallery: (Pennsylvania Avenue and 17th Street). The best of American design, crafts, and decorative arts.

Excursions from Washington, DC

Mount Vernon (VIRGINIA): (*16 miles/26km south on Mt Vernon Memorial Parkway; also by Tourmobile in summer; tel: 703-780-2000; open daily*): More than just a dutiful pilgrimage to the home of George Washington, Mount Vernon offers a journey back to an 18th-century Virginia plantation, beautifully restored, the lawns perhaps a shade more tailored than in the old days. Make the 35-minute drive early in the morning to avoid the spring and summer crowds and sit, as George and his wife Martha did, on the square-columned veranda that overlooks the tranquil Potomac River valley and the green Maryland hills in the distance.

Great soldier and leader of men, George Washington was also an accomplished farmer, one of the first to develop and apply extended crop rotation plans. He owned 8,000 acres (3,250 hectares) of land, divided into five farms, and had 120 slaves to work them. At the border of the immaculate Bowling Green, you'll pass old trees planted by George himself. Inside the house, you can see Martha's account books, each item carefully recorded. The furniture is 18th-century; George's bedroom has the original pieces, including the fine portmanteau trunk that accompanied him throughout the Revolutionary War campaign, and the bed he was in when he died in 1799.

Colonial Williamsburg

Colonial Virginia: *(South from Washington on Interstate 95 via Richmond to State Highway 5).* Highway 5 takes you through lovely plantation country to the historic triangle of Jamestown, where Virginia was founded; Williamsburg,

> **Williamsburg, Jamestown and Yorktown are three of America's most historic sites. If time is very tight, they can all be visited in the same day.**

Virginia's capital from 1699 to 1780; and Yorktown, where the Revolutionary War reached its triumphant climax in 1781. The towns are linked by the Colonial Parkway on which a Visitors Center dispenses tickets for Colonial Williamsburg (exit 238 off Interstate 64).

Colonial Williamsburg is the largest scale restoration project in the country, with over 500 meticulously restored 18th-century buildings. Visitors are invited to engage with its denizens (over 800 actors in period dress). Visit the cobbler's, gunsmith's, apothecary, and printer's workshops and learn about these crafts from the artisans, or take a horse-drawn carriage ride.

The restoration was carried out with funds from John D. Rockefeller, Jr, in 1927. Drawing on 18th-century engravings found in Oxford, England's Bodleian Library, architectural historians restored the 1705 **Capitol** building and **Governor's Palace** in precise detail. For the latter, they were aided by a plan of the interior drawn by Thomas Jefferson, who lived here for six months as Governor of Virginia. The major thoroughfare is **Duke of Gloucester Street**, with some of the finest wooden weatherboard and red-brick Georgian houses. Revolutionary bigwigs met at the Raleigh Tavern; you can taste 18th-century dishes at the King's Arms, Chowning's, and Christiana Campbell's taverns, all in fine restored state.

Jamestown, 6 miles (10km) south of Williamsburg, was the site settled by the first pioneers from London in May 1607 (13 years before the *Mayflower* reached Massachusetts). The only original relic of colonial Jamestown is a crumbling church tower. The site was abandoned because of malarial mosquitoes (gone now). But **Jamestown Festival Park** has been built as a replica of the old palisade fort, with a 17th-century pottery and a Native American ceremonial lodge. On the river are full-scale replicas of the tiny vessels *Susan Constant, Discovery,* and *Godspeed,* which brought John Smith and 103 settlers across the Atlantic Ocean on their courageous voyage. Visitors can go aboard the *Susan Constant* to witness the cramped living conditions that those travelers endured.

Yorktown, 18 miles (29km) to the east, is where Lord Cornwallis surrendered his British troops in October 1781, sealing Britain's loss of its American colonies. Before visiting the battlefield, stop at the Yorktown Victory Center, just 2 miles (3km) out of town, where you can visit a Continental Army encampment, talk to costumed interpreters, and see a display of Revolutionary War artifacts. In town, visit **Moore House**, where the British negotiated their capitulation with the Americans and the French.

The Declaration of Independence was signed in Philadelphia

Major Cities near Washington, DC

Baltimore and Philadelphia are interesting counterparts to Washington, DC. Baltimore, a major seaport for the Chesapeake Bay, has undergone an exciting urban renewal, and is a great place for seafood, while Philidelphia is the birthplace of American nationhood and has a colorful mixture of ethnic groups.

Baltimore *(MARYLAND):* Baltimore suffers from what Balti-moreans consider unfair barbs. Poet Edgar Allan Poe died here and was buried in Westminster Churchyard, but otherwise the town is somewhat lacking in historical monuments. But it makes up for this with some of the boldest urban renewal in the country. The **Charles Center** has turned the erstwhile blight of the downtown business district into a lively area of stores, theaters, and cafés. Equally successful and more attractive is the 95-acre (38-hectare) **Inner Harbor** development, which has transformed the once seedy waterfront of Baltimore Har-bor into a stylish setting for hotels, theaters, restaurants, parks, and promenades. Art shows, concerts, and sports activ-ities keep the place hopping throughout the year. The restau-rants around the harbor serve fine seafood straight from the bay – clams and oysters, soft-shell crab, crab cakes, and a Baltimore specialty, hard-shell crabs.

At Constellation Dock you can tour the restored Navy frigate *Constellation*, which was launched here in 1797. Landlubbers who prefer old locomotives can see a fine collection at the **Balti-more & Ohio Railroad Museum** (Poppleton and Pratt streets).

Pride of the **Baltimore Museum of Art** (Charles and 31st streets, tel: 410-396-7100) is the excellent Cone Collection of 19th- and 20th-century paintings, well endowed with works by Matisse and Picasso.

Philadelphia *(PENNSYLVANIA):* One of the more charming aspects of America is that this Pennsylvania town that occupies such an important place in the history of the USA should also be a national joke. Philadelphia, after all, is the City of Brotherly Love that William Penn established as a model of religious free-dom and colonial enterprise and where Benjamin Franklin and Thomas Jefferson championed the movement for independence. But it's also a quiet, sedate town – which comedian W.C. Fields unfavorably commemorated on his tombstone; 'better than play-ing Philadelphia,' and where the master of horror, Edgar Allan Poe, wrote his famous poem *The Raven*.

While the modern city has been enlivened by its Italian and Jewish communities, it's the old Anglo-Saxon backbone that sets a dignified tone. According to Mark Twain, 'In Boston, they ask 'How much does he know?' In New York, 'How much is he worth?' In Philadelphia, 'Who were his parents?'

Today the town's past is still of vital importance to its citizens. And they proudly proclaim **Independence National Historical Park** at the heart of old Philadelphia, containing all the great buildings of early America's government, as the 'most historic square mile in America.' At the grand red-brick Georgian **Independence Hall** (5th and Chestnut) you can see where America's founding fathers signed the Declaration of Independence and, later, the United States Constitution.

Next door, the states' representatives met in **Congress Hall** and signed the Bill of Rights that forced the government to protect rather than interfere with individual freedoms. In the **Liberty Bell Center** on Market Street between 5th and 6th streets is the famous **Liberty Bell** in its glass pavilion. This was the bell that came from England in 1751, cracked en route as if to symbolize the American fissure in Britain's empire, was repaired in time to ring out from the tower of Independence Hall on July 4, 1776, and cracked again in the 19th century.

The Liberty Bell

Philadelphia's original Liberty Bell was cast in England by the Whitechapel Foundry in London and delivered in 1752. It famously cracked the first time it was struck.

The same foundry was commissioned to provide an exact replacement for the bicentennial celebrations in 1976, and it now hangs in the Liberty Bell Center, bearing the inscription:

'FOR THE PEOPLE OF THE UNITED STATES OF AMERICA
FROM THE PEOPLE OF BRITAIN
4 JULY 1976
LET FREEDOM RING'

In case you still haven't grasped Philadelphians' view of their city's importance, take a look at the magnificent **City Hall** (Market and Broad streets). The Louvre in Paris was its architectural model and, locals like to point out, it's bigger than Washington's Capitol building. On top is a statue of William Penn. The **Philadelphia Museum of Art** (26th and the Parkway) houses a good collection of American works, plus some fine Impressionist (Van Gogh's *Sunflowers*) and Post-Impressionist paintings. It also has excellent special exhibitions. **Edgar Allan Poe's House** (532 North 7th Street) is now a museum of Poe memorabilia. He lived here with his young wife. The **Rodin Museum** (22nd and Parkway) has the biggest collection of the French sculptor's work outside Paris. The **Franklin Institute** (20th and Parkway) is a marvelous science museum, with halls devoted to astronomy, computers, electronics, railroads, aviation, geology, weather, biology, and Franklin's experiments with electricity. There's also an IMAX theater.

THE SOUTH

For people on vacation, the South is where the sun always shines. For Americans, it's also an almost mythical place perceived through its history – an antebellum serenity and paternalism, the blood and fire of civil war, resentments of reconstruction, and a 20th-century struggle for parity with the North and a new pride and prosperity. Parity, but not conformity.

The South has held on to an exotic quality that spices courtly mellow decadence with a hint of danger below the surface. To sort out myth and reality would require a stay of months or years, crisscrossing the Carolinas, Georgia, Florida, Alabama, Mississippi, Louisiana, and Arkansas. But for an introduction, start with Florida for the exquisite hedonism of its subtropical sun, then to Charleston, South Carolina for an echo of the golden past, over to Atlanta for a look at the 'New South,' and then to New Orleans, a grand old river city with a unique Creole flavor.

In southern Florida's subtropical climate, with air and seawater temperatures ranging from an average low of 74°F (23°C) in January to an average high of 88°F (31°C) in August, lovers of heat should watch out. Sunbathing here should begin with no more than 30 minutes the first day; the Florida sun can scorch even when the sky is overcast.

Miami and the Beaches

Miami Beach (*FLORIDA*): Connected to mainland Miami by causeways across Biscayne Bay, this is where the pleasure begins: 7 miles (11km) of sandy beaches in front of high-rise hotels and condominium apartments.

After a careful dose of sun the first day, you might like to check out the various beaches. If your hotel has commandeered its own piece of the shoreline – as is the case around 46th Street – you may be perfectly happy to stay there, but if not, there are several alternatives.

A few years ago these fine beaches nearly disappeared because of the erosion caused by undisciplined construction along the seafront. At the end of the 1970s, the US Army Corps of Engineers came to the rescue by dumping 13½ million cubic yards (10 million cubic meters) of sand along the reclaimed 100-yd (91-m) wide strip of seashore.

Haulover Beach, at the north end, is for the very active, with palm trees to shade lazy companions. It's well-known for surfing, frisbee-tossing, and fishing off the pier. There are also barbecue grills where you can turn your catch into a picnic.

Surfside at 93rd Street and the **64th and 53rd Street beaches** are best for swimming, away from the high-end crowds that parade along Miami Beach.

21st Street is a favorite with young people, who turn the fast-food stands into lively open-air clubs.

Away from the sands, Miami Beach offers architectural rewards for art-deco buffs. Along Collins Avenue and down into **South Beach** is the delightful ice-cream-cake confection of the **Art Deco District**. An entire square mile (2.5 sq. km) of the district was listed in the National Registry of Historic Places, and there are few neighborhoods anywhere more likely to put a smile on your face. Around **Washington Avenue**, on the blocks between 8th and 21st streets, you can stroll around hotels, apartment buildings, restaurants, and stores that sprang up in the tourist boom of the 1920s and 1930s, with a flourish of chrome and bakelite, gaily colored ceramic tiles and mirrored glass, borrowing motifs from the Egyptians and Aztecs. After years of scorn by purists who found the buildings too 'florid,' South Beach and the Deco District is now not only the trendiest place in Florida, but one of the major entertainment and fashion capitals in America. Dress to the hilt

Miami's art deco delights

when you go, and be sure to try a pink cocktail.

Collins Avenue stretches for many blocks of more modern hotels (i.e. 1950s), the flagship being the **Fontainebleau Hilton** at 44th Street (tel: 305-538-2000). Even if you're not staying here, plan to have a drink and a look around this unquestionable monument to American leisure. No expense has been spared in the serpentine pool, cabanas, waterfalls, grottoes, hidden bars, tennis courts, luxury stores, 10 restaurants, and aquarium to make you feel anywhere but at home. Today, everyone's a film star.

For a taste of ultra-modern chic of the South Beach variety, pay a visit to the **Delano Hotel** (1685 Collins Avenue, tel: 305-672-2000). International hotelier Ian Schrager and designer Phillipe Starck partnered to remodel this 1947 hotel with super-elegant austerity. The building itself is also distinctive, with its modernist finned tower.

Metro Miami (*FLORIDA*): Sun, sea, and sand worshippers tend to avoid the city of Miami itself, but they're missing some major attractions. Like many older residents, they got frightened by the influx of immigrants from Cuba and Haiti and the stories of drugs, voodoo, and violent crime. The stories are true – in the early 1990s, drugs were one of the four main sources of revenue in Florida, along with tourism, citrus fruits, and manufacturing. Things have calmed down, but it's still a good idea to exercise reasonable care. That said, there's plenty of fun to be had in this high-color town.

Downtown is a busy area of department stores, restaurants, and nightclubs around Flagler Street and Biscayne Boulevard. But it's even livelier south of Downtown in the Cuban neighborhood of **Little Havana**, centered on a 30-block section around 'Calle Ocho' (SW 8th Street) running east from 37th Avenue. More than a quarter of Miami's 2 million people are Cubans, and here is where they hand-roll their cigars, eat wonderful food, and dance.

Try the strong Cuban coffee, served espresso-style on the street in paper cups, or cocoa for dipping your *churro* (a long thin doughnut). At Ocho and 14th Avenue is the site of the open-air **Domino Park**, where neighborhood enthusiasts (male only, women just watch) play chess with a concentration worthy of a grand-master. On SW 9th Street is the **Juan J. Peruyero Museum** and the **Manuel F. Artime Library**, both named after Cuban leaders who are now dead. This is a fascinating place, well worth a look. The rooms are filled with maps, photographs, and old newpaper clippings dating back to the early 1960s. On Ocho and 12th Avenue, you can watch cigars being rolled, pressed, wrapped, and cut with elegant dexterity.

The closest thing Miami has to an artists' quarter is a place called **Coconut Grove** (South Bay Shore Drive), which is a pleasant self-contained community of boutiques, galleries, and parks, with stylish sailing boats bobbing in the harbor. Coconut Grove and South Beach are the two places to stay if you don't want to have to rent a car.

Across the Rickenbacker Causeway, **Key Biscayne** has delightful beaches at Bill Baggs Cape Florida State Recreation Area. But the star of Miami's many wildlife attractions is the **Miami Seaquarium** (tel: 305-361-5705), just off the causeway on Virginia Key. Here you'll find whales, dolphins, sharks, and turtles at play, eating, and in languid repose. The dolphins leap any height for a few fish and the spectators' delight. Seaquarium is one of the few places where you can see the rare manatee, or sea cow, a large seal-like mammal that used to live in great numbers in Florida's waterways. And in **Parrot Jungle**, on Parrot Jungle Trail, the birds perform more tricks than the dolphins – riding bicycles, roller-skating, even doing arithmetic. The flamingos alone are worth it.

But man remains the most fascinating trickster. Look at what industrialist James Deering did with his **Vizcaya** home (3251 South Miami Avenue, tel: 305-250-9133). This 70-room Renaissance-style *palazzo* on Biscayne Bay opulently displays almost every artistic style that western man produced, from the

Miami beach life

AD200 altar to the 1915 gold plumbing fixtures. The formal gardens are bizarrely beautiful and the barge in the harbor is made of stone, a sculpture by A. Stirling Calder, less mobile than the works done later by his son Alexander.

In 1925, **St Bernard's Monastery** (16711 West Dixie Highway, off Biscayne Boulevard) was shipped from Segovia in Spain – stone by numbered stone – in 11,000 crates. It had been bought by William Randolph Hearst, who intended to use it to house a swimming pool on his estate in California *(see page 179)*. Unfortunately, the crates were packed with hay that the US Department of Agriculture deemed a health hazard to animals (there had been foot-and-mouth disease in Segovia), so the dismantled monastery stayed on the East Coast. Bought and reassembled by a local entrepreneur, it is now under the auspices of the Episcopal Diocese of South Florida. The choral recitals are a deliciously anachronistic experience.

Lastly, the **Holocaust Memorial** (Meridian Avenue and Dade Boulevard) features a devastating sculptural tribute to the Holocaust's 6 million victims, *The Sculpture of Love and Anguish*. Forged by sculptor Kenneth Treister, this 42-ft (13-m) high bronze arm bears an Auschwitz tattoo number and smaller bronze figures scaling its surface. Combining historical exhibits, photographs, and other sculptural monuments, the memorial prompts an elegiac moment of quiet reflection.

The Everglades

The watery plain known as the Everglades (toll road south to Homestead, then take State Route 27; follow signs to the National Park) has given swamps a good name as wonderlands of natural beauty. A 50-mile (80-km) band of brackish water from Lake Okeechobee flows lazily through Florida to the ocean. Called the 'River of Grass,' the slow-moving bog teems with wildlife. The **Everglades National Park** covers nearly half a million acres (more than 200,000 hectares) under the protection of US Rangers. The rangers, stationed at visitor centers throughout the park, advise on how to enjoy – and not spoil – the wilderness.

From the park entrance southwest of Homestead (pick up a map at the Visitor Center), the road runs 38 miles (61km) to the western Gulf Coast. Marked turnoffs take you to campgrounds and picnic areas beside lakes or near 'hammocks' – raised areas in the swamps. The first turnoff leads to the **Royal Palm Visitor Center** on the edge of a freshwater slough. In the clear waters of the pond you will see shoals of fish, among them the Florida garfish, enjoyed by alligators. You can watch one of the short slide shows at the Visitor Center before taking the Anhinga and Gumbo Limbo foot-trails.

The Anhinga Trail's raised boardwalk circles over sawgrass marsh where you can see alligators, egrets, herons, and the snake-bird. The Gumbo Limbo is a circular half-mile (1-km) track through jungle vegetation. Watch for raccoons, opossums, tree snails, and lizards, which are very common around these parts.

At the end of the main road is **Flamingo**, a fishing town on a shallow bay dotted with islands. In the good old days, it pro-

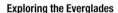

Exploring the Everglades

duced illicit 'moonshine' alcohol. Now it's a tourist center with a motel, housekeeping cabins, and a campground. At the Flamingo Marina you can rent tackle, boats, and canoes to fish for trout, redfish, snapper, and snook (which has a taste like pike). Find your own way up to **Everglades City** through a chain of lakes and rivers called 'The Wilderness Waterway,' or take a sightseeing boat from Flamingo. The abundant wildlife on the coast and in the interior includes ibises, ospreys, white herons, bald eagles, snowy egrets, otters, roseate spoonbills, green turtles, manatees (the gentle 'sea cows' increasingly threatened by fast motorboats), and rare Florida panthers. Coat yourself in insect repellent and be sure to follow the rangers' advised precautions about poisonous plants and snakes.

The Gold Coast

The 70-mile (113-km) long Gold Coast north of Miami offers half a dozen vacation resorts favored by those escaping the winter rigors of New York, New England, the Midwest, and Canada. Hotels and condominiums gleam white across wide, palm-tree–lined boulevards that border on spotless beaches.

Fort Lauderdale: This beach town is crazy. Its peak moment of madness is the month-long Easter vacation when roughly a quarter of a million sun-starved students from the North descend on the town. Early evening, the teenagers cruise their cars bumper to bumper up and down the A1A 'Strip' along the seafront. Summer and winter, the town settles down as private boats and yachts (estimated to number 30,000 on and off the canals) drift along the network of inland waterways past elegant marina homes. The best way to view them – if you're not thinking of chartering a yacht – is to take one of the paddle-boat cruises from the Bahia Mar marina.

Boca Raton: This elegant town is lazy. It's the winter home of a highly regarded polo club, but you can also enjoy the wonderful beaches tucked behind the dunes. Or rent a rod and pretend to fish off the rocks around the inlet. If you must be active, go birding or hiking around Deerfield Island Park, once the home of Chicago mobster Al Capone.

Palm Beach: The place that put the 'gold' in the Gold Coast. (The palms in Palm Beach are said to have grown from coconuts spilled in a Spanish shipwreck.) The town was created after oil and railroad magnate Henry Flagler was persuaded at the end of the 19th century that Florida's warm winters made the state a

In wealthy Palm Beach it is against the law to park almost anywhere, to own a kangaroo or any other exotic animal, or to hang a clothesline. Tourists are tolerated in this mainly residential town, as long as they keep a low profile.

viable proposition for his railroad expansion. At the same time as the railroad was being built down the Gold Coast, the secluded location of Palm Beach struck Flagler as just the kind of place for his kind of person. Now one of America's wealthiest communities, it stretches its splendid *palazzi* along Ocean Boulevard, not far from the proprietors' yachts in the harbor. You can catch glimpses of these opulent residences as you wind through the impeccable landscaping. Flagler's own home is on Coconut Row, a white marble palace named Whitehall, now the **Flagler Museum** (tel: 561-655-2833; open daily, Sun pm only). Its 55 opulently restored rooms trace the town's early history amid elegant old furnishings, including the master's private railway car.

In this, Florida's ultimate consumer paradise, there is scarcely a luxury store of the world that is not represented on the pride and joy of Palm Beach: **Worth Avenue**. It's a street that ranks alongside Paris's Rue du Faubourg St-Honoré or London's Bond Street. Even if your budget doesn't allow you to go wild and buy all the elegant goodies you want, you can still press your nose against the windows. You'll notice that the couturiers go a little crazy in the colors they choose here. It's the Florida sun that does it. You'll also see the most delightfully flamboyant golfing clothes ever offered. What's more, there are people actually wearing them on this hallowed avenue. The Gucci store is worth the detour – it's nothing less than a Florentine *palazzo*, with fountains playing in the tree-shaded courtyard.

➤ **Kennedy Space Center:** Located about 100 miles (160km) to the north on Merritt Island, this is the site of all US manned-craft launchings. Unmanned flights are launched from Cape Canaveral, across the Banana River. An ideal trip here would include watching a launching, but since the tragedy in February, 2003 – when the space shuttle *Columbia* exploded upon re-entry into the earth's atmosphere killing all seven astronauts – the launch program has been put back. Information about dates and possible reservations can be made by calling 407-452-2121. Otherwise there's still plenty to see, especially if you avoid the crowds by arriving early at the Visitors Center on State Route 405 and catch one of the two-hour bus tours.

Seventeen tours and attractions are on offer. As well as the bus tour, these include walk-through exhibits on exploration and early space travel; the space station module; robotic space explorers; the *Apollo-Soyuz* command module; the moon rocket; an observation tower; the launch status ('mission control') center; an IMAX theater, and two wildlife refuges.

Orlando

➤ **Walt Disney World Resort:** *(20 miles/32km southwest of Orlando off Interstate 4 and State Highway 192. For more information, including Disney's wide range of accommodations, contact Walt Disney World, PO Box 10000, Lake Buena Vista, FL 32830, or <www.disneyworld.com>).* With Walt Disney World, the grand old moviemaker's company has turned his fantasies into a mammoth holiday resort development, with its own hotels, campgrounds, golf courses, water theme parks, boating facilities, vacation villas, and stores, surrounding some of the biggest theme parks in the world. The area covers 43 sq. miles (111 sq. km) – much of it reclaimed marshland.

Unless you have bought a package that includes entrance fees, you can choose between an annual ticket and a myriad of other type tickets, from one-day to a week or more. The days don't have to be consecutive, and once you're inside, all rides and exhibits are free. A 'Fastpass' ticket cuts down on the excrutiatingly long waiting lines. At each park entrance, be sure to pick up a map and a timetable.

The Magic Kingdom: Once past the ticket booths, choose between the ultra-modern monorail or the more leisurely ferryboat across the lake to the Magic Kingdom's entrance. Now you're in fairyland, with Cinderella's castle, and surrounded by Mickey Mouse and a host of Disney movie characters. Take your choice of the Kingdom's many different sections.

Enjoying the Disney magic

Main Street, USA, is the very symbol of the good old American way of life, from the entrance under the Train Station past gabled and turreted turn-of-the-19th-century buildings to Town Square, where City Hall dispenses information about the rest of the Magic Kingdom and Walt Disney World in general.

Adventureland proposes exotic tropical flora and fauna. A gigantic (concrete) banyan tree supporting the Swiss Family Robinson Treehouse stands by the landing stage for the Jungle Cruise, complete with trailing vines and (foam-rubber) wild animals. Frontierland romanticizes the pioneer days. Splash Mountain is a log flume ride with a drenching finale, while Big Thunder Mountain Railroad is a roller coaster in an elaborate red-rock setting.

Liberty Square doesn't quite replace a visit to New England but makes a valiant effort to capture the atmosphere of the Republic's cradle at Liberty Tree Tavern. The big attraction, though, is the Haunted Mansion.

Fantasyland takes you on a submarine voyage 20,000 Leagues Under the Sea or on a dizzying whirl in the Mad Hat-

Epcot's disinctive dome

ter's gigantic teacup. Every childhood character seems to be here – Peter Pan, Snow White's Seven Dwarfs, and Disney's own Mickey Mouse.

Mickey's Toontown Fair is a 3-acre (1-hectare) extravaganza with sections devoted to Goofy, Minnie, and the main mouse, Mickey. Check out the interactive lily pads.

Tomorrowland is devoted to space technology and sci-fi. You can go on a Mission to Mars or pilot a Star-Jet. Space Mountain hides a heart-stopping simulated space ride. The ExtraTERRORestrial Alien Encounter is a sci-fi scarefest. Even some adults might find it a little intense.

Epcot Center: Out of Walt Disney's last dreams of an Experimental Prototype Community of Tomorrow is one of his company's most ambitious entertainment centers, south of the Magic Kingdom. The park presents the past and future of our planet, together with a showcase of some of the world's nations, all within a few hundred acres around an artificial lake. Every night there is a spectacular firework display over the lake.

In **Future World**, a monorail takes you around polygonal, spherical, dome-shaped, or pyramidal pavilions (each sponsored by a major American company) demonstrating the evolution of our civilization and the new technologies that will be tomorrow's tools. The centerpiece is Spaceship Earth, a 180-ft (55-m) high, white geosphere. Other attractions include the **Universe of Energy** and the **Wonders of Life**, including Body Wars, a simulator ride that sends you on a frenetic journey through the human body. The other part of Epcot is **World Showcase**, which presents different nations through their monuments, landmarks, and cuisines.

Disney-MGM Studios: More like 1930s Hollywood, probably, than Hollywood ever was, the art-deco streets of this theme park lead to real and replica film sets. You'll see stunt shows, ride through movie history, meet the Muppets, and learn some of the secrets of Walt Disney's animation techniques. *Fastasmic* is a nightly show that dazzles the audience with lasers, fountains and fireballs. The big draw around **Echo Lake** is the Indiana Jones Epic Stunt Spectacular.

Disney's Animal Kingdom: This park, the largest of all the parks, is essentially a state-of-the-art zoo dressed up in extravagant style. As well as live shows like the Festival of the Lion King, based loosely on the animated film, there are nature walks where you can view endangered species like black-and-white colobus monkeys and hippos, gorillas and meerkats.

Two water parks complete the Disney City: Blizzard Beach, the largest and the newest, and Typhoon Lagoon.

Jaws recreated at Universal

To see some of the highlights of all the parks, you'll need at least a week, maybe even more. You'll walk miles and miles and there's a lot of waiting in line when the parks are at their busiest. This is particularly tiring on a hot summer's day (the most popular months are June to August), although you can rent strollers (pushchairs) and wheelchairs.

➤ **Universal Studios Orlando:** *(tel: 407-363-8000):* Film and TV fans can relive some of their favorite movies and see new productions in progress. Hundreds of millions of dollars have been spent to create thrilling special-effects rides,

rides, and some real, some look-alike stars make an appearance. Make sure you arrive early in the day in order to find out about any special events that might be planned. You'll need to spend most of the day here: one- and two-day tickets are available.

There's a lot of walking, though strollers and wheelchairs can be rented. **Islands of Adventure** is a recent Universal theme park, five elaborately themed zones arrayed around a central lagoon ; the high-tech thrill rides are particularly impressive.

Elsewhere in the South

Charleston (*SOUTH CAROLINA*): Standing aloof at the point where the Ashley and Cooper rivers flow together into the Atlantic Ocean, this town evokes that elegant, courtly atmosphere that people still associate with the 'Old South.' After South Carolina led the southern states' secession from the Union, Charleston was the town that fired the first shots in the Civil War. Ever since, it has maintained, with winning self-consciousness, the South's distinctively well-mannered sense of dignified separateness.

Charleston's Historic District includes over 2,000 buildings. You might start at **The Battery**, curving up to East Bay Street, where antebellum houses snake along narrow shaded cobblestone streets surrounded by gardens of dogwood, wisteria, and azalea. Running west from East Bay Street is Market Street, which leads to attractive **Market Square**. Here, open-air cafés, restaurants, art galleries, and boutiques have been installed in renovated warehouses – very much in keeping with the nationwide movement for redeveloping derelict downtown neighborhoods. It's a great place to have lunch, and watch the people and the fascinating workings of this charming city.

From the Municipal Marina at the junction of Calhoun Street and Lockwood Drive on the west (Ashley River) side of the peninsula, you can take a boat trip out to historic **Fort Sumter**. This is the old military base that, during the Civil War, was wrested from the United States Army by the South Carolina militia in April 1861, to the polite applause of the

Charleston gentry assembled on the harbor. It was recaptured, after a two-year siege, in February 1865. The two-hour boat cruise includes a visit to the Civil War Museum and a tour of the remains of the fort. Call (843) 722-2628 for reservations.

Sweet song of the South

Two excursions out of town will take you back to the antebellum days of the cotton plantations. **Boone Hall,** (7 miles/11km north on Highway 17, tel: 843-884-4371), a restored 18th-century plantation home and grounds, is said to have been used as the Tara Plantation for the filming of *Gone with the Wind*. But the more spectacular grounds are at beautiful **Magnolia Gardens** (tel: 843-571-1266), located 14 miles (23km) north of Charleston on Highway 61. This lovely 400-acre (160-hectare) nature reserve, once a huge plantation established in 1676, combines exotic flora with fine opportunities to immerse yourself in nature, including birding, hiking, cycling, and canoeing.

Atlanta (*GEORGIA*): This historic capital of Georgia is also the bold and busy capital of the New South. The town's symbol, which you can see in two fine sculptures – one on Broad Street by the First National Bank, the other on Martin Luther King Drive – is the phoenix, the mythical bird that rose from its own ashes. The town's modern prosperity was spurred by its total destruction in 1864 during the Civil War. Two years later it was the federal headquarters for the South's Reconstruction, and its dynamism is still intact.

Venue for the 1996 Olympic Games, the town has brave contemporary architecture, elegant stores, smart restaurants, and lively nightclubs – the backdrop to a town combining Yankee sophistication with the savvy of those redneck good ol' boys who sometimes sound as if they just hit town, and hit it hard.

To get an ideal overview, start your tour with a trip to the 70th-floor revolving restaurant on top of the **Peachtree Plaza Hotel** – the elevators whiz up through glass tubes on the outside of the building. The view is spectacular, on a clear day you can see all the way to the Blue Ridge Mountains in North Carolina.

Linked to the plaza, **Peachtree Center** is the heart of Downtown, an airy shopping and business center with attractive landscaping among the skyscrapers, drooping vines and tropical plants, reflecting pools, and splashing fountains. Even if you're not staying there, be sure to visit the Hyatt Regency Hotel, a pioneer in modern atrium architecture: the skyscraper is built around a skylit courtyard with its own café-terrace inside the hotel.

The **Martin Luther King, Jr National Historic Site** along Auburn Avenue NE includes several facilities: the Visitor Center (at No. 450) features exhibits from M.L.K.'s life and the progress of the Civil Rights movement; the King Center (No. 449) is an institute for social change, where M.L.K.'s tomb is located; the Ebenezer Baptist Church (No. 407) is where M.L.K. and his father preached their message of non-violence. The King Birth Home (No. 501) can be visited with a guided tour.

One fine testimony to Atlanta's entrepreneurial energy is the **Omni International Complex** (100 Techwood Drive), a dazzling 34-acre (14-hectare) megastructure, as Atlantans like to call it, containing a sports coliseum for ice hockey, basketball, circuses, and concerts, and a convention center with movie theaters, stores, nightclubs, a skating rink, and restaurants. Multicolored laser beams light up the enormous interior at night, while hundreds of 'sun sculpture' prisms set in the skylight create a charming kaleidoscopic effect by day.

The **High Museum of Art** (Peachtree and 16th streets, tel: 404-577-6940) is a stunning white building with an excellent collection of American decorative art, African art, and fine modern paintings. Its folk art and photography collections are worth a look, too.

Atlanta is the home base of Coca-Cola, and the company's family-friendly **World of Coca-Cola** gives a fascinating glimpse into the history and advertising of this bubbly symbol of Americana. Free drinks are offered and there's a good gift shop. **Underground Atlanta** is an entertainment complex in the heart of the city. Atlanta is also home to CNN-TV, and 45-minute tours (tel: (404) 827-2300) of the studios at the gigantic CNN **Center** on Marietta Street provide fascinating glimpses into a newsroom in full swing.

The French Quarter, New Orleans

New Orleans (*LOUISIANA*): Whatever is exotic, lurid, even sinful in the popular image of the South stems in large part from this port town at the mouth of the Mississippi River. In New Orleans, the jazz that grew up in its brothels and steamy saloons is still hot, and the Creole cooking brought from the West Indies by the old French and Spanish settlers even hotter. You'll find them both in the French Quarter. And if the elegant decadence of the antebellum aristocracy is at best a whispered legend handed down to a few strutting diehards, take a look at their granddaddies' splendid Greek Revival townhouses in the Garden District and you'll see what a proud world they lost when they had to give up their slaves. Mississippi gamblers no longer fleece wealthy widows on riverboats coming all the way down from Natchez, but the sternwheeler steamboats are back in service again for cruises along Ol' Man River.

Mardi Gras is made for floats and fancy costumes

The closest they get to being exotic, lurid, and sinful these days is at the great Mardi Gras carnival (usually February or March), so successful that the city fathers are now turning every imaginable occasion – Halloween, St Patrick's Day, the arrival of spring or summer – into another festival, however hot and humid it may get. New Orleans loves parades, but if they haven't found an excuse for one when you're visiting, you'll still find a public party going on somewhere, and with all the trumpets and trombones blowing full blast, it won't be hard to find.

French Quarter: Known locally as the Vieux Carré (Old Square), this is the historic heart of town, bounded by Canal and Rampart streets (the latter originally a fortification), Esplanade Avenue, and the Mississippi River. Great fires in 1788 and 1794 destroyed over 1,000 houses in the quarter, but the 19th-century reconstruction has maintained the old two- and three-story houses with filigreed wrought-iron galleries providing the roof for shaded colonnades at street level. This, despite the encroachment of new hotels and saloons, remains the quarter's dominant architecture.

Start at **Jackson Square** where, around the statue of General Andrew Jackson, there is bustle all day long with clowns, magicians, balloon-vendors, and assorted eccentrics sporting strange costumes. Groups of children stage tap-dancing shows on street corners, embedding bottle caps in the soles and heels of their sneakers to provide the 'tap.' Flanking the cathedral are two relics of the colonial era – the **Cabildo**, originally a police station and later the City Hall, and the **Presbytère**, a priests' residence that became a courthouse. They are now part of the **Louisiana State Museum**.

The Cabildo's exhibits tell the often-exciting history of trade on the Mississippi, while the Presbytère houses cultural displays that aptly illustrate the area's rich history through the use of photographs and maps. **St Louis Cathedral** is an 1851 restoration of the 18th-century church of the French Catholic diocese, more famous for the duels in its garden than for its architecture. Around the square are the two rows of the **Pontalba Buildings**, with elegant wrought-ironwork on the upper-story galleries.

Walk down Dumaine Street past Madame John's Legacy, a preserved French colonial cottage, to Royal Street, one of the most

Carnival Time

Shrove Tuesday, the British call it, but people in the US translate the French as 'Fat Tuesday,' a last hedonistic fling before Lenten austerity. It's New Orleans' great moment of madness, bringing hundreds of thousands of revelers – be sure to book your hotel room months in advance – for the parade of floats down St Charles Avenue, and others throughout the city. The King of Rex, the star of the main parade, is a local businessman, while the King of Bacchus, whose parade is two days earlier, is always a celebrity.

Private masked balls start on Twelfth Night (January 6), and the parades start 11 days before Mardi Gras. Although Mardi Gras takes place in February or early March, the weather is usually delightfully balmy.

Hot jazz in a cool town

gracious in the quarter, awash with high-class antiques shops. To the right, at 1132 Royal Street, the **Gallier House**, named after its architect, James Gallier, is one of the few authentic old New Orleans houses now open to the public. It has been restored to its original 1857 condition, and if you walk out on the wrought-iron balcony you get a view of the neighborhood's old tranquillity. This is an intellectual respite before venturing out to attack the hurly-burly of **Bourbon Street's** saloons.

If you want to save Bourbon Street till night, hop aboard one of the modern riverfront streetcars for a ride along the Mississippi. *A Streetcar Named Desire*, the play by Tennessee Williams, made this type of local transportation famous. Desire is in fact the name of a street a dozen or so blocks east of here, and that streetcar doesn't run anymore, but you can still take the original St Charles Avenue streetcar through the Garden District and back starting from Carondelet at Canal. Plans are afoot to install more streetcar lines throughout the city sometime around 2005. This is an excellent idea, as locals as well as tourists hop on and off these eco-friendly vehicles several times a day.

Back in the quarter and close to the waterfront is the **French Market**. Here boutiques and souvenir shops segue into a covered produce and condiment market, alternating with many open-air restaurants providing the theme music of New Orleans – live jazz – and leading to a bustling flea market.

The ever-popular 24-hour **Café du Monde** near Jackson Square serves delicious *café au lait* and *beignets* (doughnuts), on a very Gallic terrace. The **Riverwalk**, on the site of the 1984 World's Fair (other side of Canal Street), is a fine mall complex right on the river.

Garden District: Southwest of the French Quarter, bordered by Magazine Street and Louisiana, St Charles, and Jackson avenues, is the Garden District. This is where the new American cotton and sugar aristocracy built their townhouses after the Louisiana Purchase, while the Creoles stayed on in the Vieux Carré. Surrounded by gardens of magnolias, oaks, and palm trees, the mansions (most not open to the public) rival outlying plantation homes. There are some particularly fine examples along **Prytania Street**.

The district's golden era ended with the double blow of the Civil War and the elimination of the Mississippi steamboat trade by the railroads. The steamboats have now been restored to service for **river tours**, starting from Toulouse Street Wharf or the Canal Street docks. Most of the cruises take you past **Chalmette National Historical Park** (also an easy 10-mile/16-km drive southeast on Route 46). Andrew Jackson's crushing victory here over the British in 1815 in the Battle of New Orleans came after a peace treaty had been signed, but it was enough to give him the national fame that won him the White House 14 years later.

All that Jazz

Cotton is no longer king, but jazz has returned to its throne in New Orleans. The once disreputable music is now officially honored in the 14-acre (6-hectare) Louis Armstrong Park on the edge of the French Quarter, and documented in the Jazz Museum in the Old Mint on Esplanade Avenue. The fabulous New Orleans Jazz and Heritage Festival is the largest music festival in the world (last weekend in April and the first weekend in May).

Jazz began at the end of the 19th century when African-American marching bands played for every social event, especially funerals, and swung all the way home, stopping in at bars and dance halls along the way. Today the action is on Bourbon, Decatur, and Frenchmen streets, shaking that rhythm more loudly than ever.

Paddlesteamers still ply the Mississippi River

If you care to end your visit with an antebellum adventure, paddlesteamers set sail several times a day from the wharf at the foot of Canal Street. Cruises can be as brief as a three-hour tour around the area, as delightful as a dinner cruise complete with Dixieland band, or as wicked as a 10-day voyage, which floats along the Mississippi River through beautiful riverports like Natchez and Memphis all the way to St Louis, Missouri in the Midwest.

THE MIDWEST

Americans who work hard bring a lot of energy and imagination to their leisure, too. Foreign visitors are often surprised at how attractive life can be in America's busiest cities – and few are busier than those of the Midwest. The area, popularly known as the Heartland, is the industrial and agricultural core of the US, covering the states of Ohio, Indiana, Illinois, Michigan, Wisconsin, Minnesota, Iowa, Missouri, Kansas, and Nebraska. From the Great Lakes across the prairies to the Great Plains, the Midwest is dominant in dairy and pig farming, corn and wheat, but it is also a flourishing industrial center specializing in steel, rubber, and car manufacture.

Chicago is the transportation hub of the continent, main junction for the national railroad system, and today blessed – one might even say cursed – with the world's busiest airport. In the neighboring state of Michigan, it's still an economic truth that if car-capital Detroit sneezes, America catches cold. These two cities have achieved their industrial and commercial preeminence with a rich and fascinating ethnic mix that makes them vibrant centers of cultural activity, too.

Chicago (*ILLINOIS*)

Braced against the shores of Lake Michigan, Chicago is a brash town with a proud urban identity. Often called America's second city, second that is to New York, this is the birthplace of legends of the Mob, the electric blues and, reputedly, the pizza. H.L. Mencken called Chicago 'the literary capital of the United States,' and writers from Nelson Algren to Nobel prizewinner Saul Bellow have been keepers of the flame. The Chicago comedy troupe 'Second City Players' spawned Steve Martin, John Belushi, Dan Aykroyd, and the *Saturday Night Live* TV show. Chicago's nickname of 'the windy city' is attributed to both the filibustering techniques of Chicago politicians (defeating bills by talking them out past their allotted time) and to the boastful promotions for the 1893 Columbian Exposition. The town does also does draw very chilly winds from the lake.

A juxtaposition of styles

A delightful surprise for many first-time visitors is the 15-mile (24-km) stretch of sandy beaches and green parkland along the lakefront

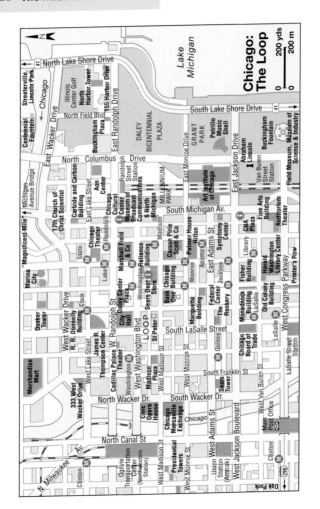

Chicago: The Loop

of this resolutely commercial city. Unlike other cities on the Great Lakes, Chicago reserved most of the land along the lakeshore for parks and residential neighborhoods, and did not allow factories. This means plenty of opportunities to sunbathe, swim, or go fishing, just a couple of blocks from the major centers of town.

The city that showed the world how to build skyscrapers learned the technique from necessity. In 1871, a fire swept through the largely wood-built town – scarcely 30 years old – leaving 100,000 homeless. Chicago had to rebuild in a hurry, with new fire-proof structures making maximum use of available ground space. The architects who worked out how to construct a building around a metal skeleton, so that it could 'go as high as you like' but with elegance and style, became collectively known around the world as the Chicago School.

They included Louis Sullivan, Daniel Burnham, and later Mies van der Rohe. Frank Lloyd Wright also worked in the Chicago area, but is better represented by his residential architecture.

Their works and those of their pupils have made of Chicago a veritable museum of modern architecture, lived-in and worked-in. In quality of design, architectural critics insist, the more famous Manhattan skyline is in no way superior to the urban panoramas along Chicago's lakefront and the downtown area.

The population of Chicago was recorded as just under 3 million in the 2001 census – a big town by any standards, but still a long way behind New York, giving an occasionally defensive air to the 'Second City,' but also acting as a spur to achievement. It was inevitable that the town's proud architectural tradition would prompt it one day to build something higher than New York's pinnacles and, sure enough, the Sears Tower held rank as the world's tallest building until it was out-distanced in 1996 by the soaring Petronas Towers in Kuala Lumpur, Malaysia.

The Chicago Symphony is one of the world's great orchestras and the Art Institute is a museum of international renown. But the people themselves, rather than aspiring to the sophistication of

Manhattanites, have a distinctively warm and cheerfully sardonic attitude to life that makes them much more approachable in public places. The old image of gangland machine-gunnings is hard to live down, but you'll not find any monuments to Al Capone, and the Mafia is no more influential here than in any other wealthy American city. There's an Anglo-Saxon business establishment, but the public tone is set much more by the Irish, Polish, German, Italian, African-American, and Jewish segments of the population.

The Chicago Transit Authority (CTA) runs a very efficient bus system, and taxis are not too expensive, but for once we recommend renting a car to move around the city, except in the congested downtown area, if you're staying more than a day. Orientation is easy: the city center is known as the Loop, after the elevated railroad track that loops around the downtown business district immediately south of the Chicago River. The other neighborhoods are defined in geographical relation to the Loop – North Side, South Side, and West Side.

Downtown Chicago seen from Lake Michigan

Michigan Avenue: Instead of starting in the hurly-burly of Downtown, we suggest you first take stock of the city from its most elegant street, certainly busy, but more measured in its pace. Chicagoans call the tree-lined stretch north of the Loop and the river up to Oak Street the **Magnificent Mile**. It contains

> William Wrigley, Jr moved to Chicago in 1891 to do business selling soap and baking powder. He gave away chewing gum to his customers, but when he saw how popular it was, he started to make and sell his own.

the town's smartest high-fashion boutiques, jewelry stores, department stores, art galleries, and bookstores. Its image is such that when McDonald's fast-food chain (corporate headquarters: Chicago) wanted to open a branch here, neighboring merchants insisted that the decor be appropriate to the location.

The result is a dignified hamburger stand indeed. The dominant landmark is the gigantic black-steel 100-story **John Hancock Center** with its dramatic exterior – a diagonally strutted skeleton. This is a vertical street unto itself, soaring 1,107ft (337.5m) into the air. The first five floors are taken up with stores, then there are half a dozen floors for parking, and above that the building has offices and apartments, with a supermarket and a swimming pool for the residents. From the 94th-floor observatory you have a view across to the Michigan shores of the lake, down over the Loop to the steel mills of Indiana, up the lakefront toward Wisconsin, and out across the flat residential neighborhoods of the West Side. Above or below, the effect of the Hancock Center is like Chicago itself, vigorous, tough, yet beautiful, too.

One block west of North Michigan, **Rush Street** is a lively entertainment area with outdoor cafés, nightclubs, restaurants, and taverns that come alive after dark. At Chicago Avenue and Michigan is a strange white-limestone turret that is, in fact, the city's most cherished historic monument, the **Water Tower**. It was built in 1869 to house a pumping-station to take water from the lake, and was the only public building to survive the Great

Picasso sculpture in front of the Richard J. Daley Center

Chicago Fire. Today it is surrounded by a pleasant park.

Water Tower Place (845 North Michigan) is an attractive shopping center with waterfalls playing alongside the escalators that carry you up seven floors of stores and restaurants. Four blocks south, **Ontario Street** is 'gallery row' for a thriving contemporary art scene.

Just before you reach the river, you might pause to take a view of one of the city's more bizarre skyscrapers. The cathedral-like **Tribune Tower** has remarkable pseudo-Gothic pinnacles and porch, and 30 storeys in between them. Built in 1925 for the *Chicago Tribune* newspaper, it was the successful entry in America's most famous architectural competition. Many of the world's leading architects – a total of 233 entries from 23 countries – submitted designs, with the Bauhaus master Walter Gropius and the great Finnish designer Eero Saarinen, among the unsuccessful entrants. Having persuaded the world by default that modern buildings should henceforth have modern designs, the tower became a unique and even lovable eccentricity.

There is an excellent ensemble view of the varied skyscraper styles around the vicinity of the Chicago River from **Michigan Avenue Bridge**. The white terra-cotta, clock-towered building just north of the bridge is the **Wrigley** of chewing-gum fame, which is particularly attractive when floodlit at night.

West along the river are the twin towers of **Marina City**, resembling two huge corncobs. The circular concrete towers, with apartments shaped like slices of pie on the upper floors, go all the way down to the rivers edge. They provide mooring spaces for 500 residents' boats, or the many businesspeople who commute to work by motorboat from the lake's North Shore suburbs. Providing a stark contrast behind them is the black-steel-and-glass monolithic slab of Mies van der Rohe's landmark IBM **Building**.

The Loop: With the 'El' (elevated railroad) rattling around its periphery of Wabash Avenue, Lake, Wells, and Van Buren streets, the Loop unmistakably means business. LaSalle Street, the heart of the financial and banking district, has the same canyon-like quality as New York's Wall Street. The major Downtown department stores are on State Street and Wabash Avenue. One of them, **Carson, Pirie & Scott**, is a mecca for architectural scholars attracted, like the earliest shoppers in 1899, by Louis Sullivan's incredibly intricate ironwork ornament over the Madison Street entrance, as well as by the then-revolutionary horizontally elongated windows.

But the most successful feature of Chicago's business district is the space devoted on its many open plazas to monumental

---

Bar Talk and the Great Fire of 1871

It has been established that the Great Fire of Chicago began in the stable of Patrick and Catherine O'Leary over on the West Side on the evening of October 8, 1871. Then Chicago bar legend takes over to insist – and it's not wise to question stories told in a Chicago bar – that it was all the fault of Mrs O'Leary's cow kicking over a paraffin lamp. At any rate, history does record that the fire raged for 27 hours, wiping out over 17,000 buildings, and when a rainstorm put it out, not only was the Water Tower still standing, but – fact, not legend – so was Mrs O'Leary's stable.

modern sculpture and mosaics rather than statues of famous men. This **plaza art**, as it has become known, began with Picasso's great *Sculpture* (1967) in front of the Richard J. Daley Center (Washington and Dearborn streets), a complex of court-house and local government buildings named after the late mayor. Like the elegant skyscraper courthouse, the 50-ft (15-m) sculpture is made of CorTen steel that weathers to the color of rust, but without the corrosion. To people who want to know whether the sculpture is to be understood as a woman or a horse, Picasso himself said they might just as well 'try to understand the song of a bird.' At any rate it draws to the plaza a constant flow of admirers and locals who just like to eat their sandwiches around it.

Other notable pieces of plaza art are Chagall's *Four Seasons*, a 70-ft (21.5-m) long mosaic on the First National Plaza (Monroe and Dearborn streets); a 53-ft (16-m) high bright red *Flamingo Stabile* by Alexander Calder (Adams and Dearborn streets), grac-ing what is regarded as the most elegant set of US Government buildings in the country, the **Federal Center**, designed by Mies van der Rohe; and, perhaps the most provocative, pop-artist Claes

---

Beethoven on the Lawn

Among the Windy City's many achievements, few are more respected than the world-famous Chicago Symphony Orchestra, where the late George Solti was one of a long series of distinguished European res-ident conductors.

Tickets for their autumn and winter concerts at Orchestra Hall (220 South Michigan) are difficult to get, but if you know well in advance when you'll be in Chicago, you can write directly to Orchestra Hall for program details and reservations.

In summer, it's slightly easier to get tickets, when the orchestra plays at Ravinia Park in the northern suburb of Highland Park. Here you can listen to their music and that of other major performers at this summer festival on the lawn while having a traditional 'Ravinia pic-nic' of chicken, strawberries, and wine.

Oldenburg's filigreed *Batcolumn*, a 100-ft (30.5-m) high baseball-bat made of 1,608 pieces of welded steel (just outside the Loop at the Social Security Administration Building, 600 West Madison Street).

Water Tower

On the edge of the Loop is the **Sears Tower** (Wacker Drive and Adams Street), which with its 110 floors rising 1,454ft (443m) in the air, was once the tallest building in the world. Actually the building consists of nine towers packed together, as its designers Skidmore, Owings & Merrill suggest, like squared cigarettes. They pop out of their packet at different heights. The structure's steel frame is sheathed in black aluminium with 16,000 bronze-tinted windows. Then there's the 103rd-floor **Skydeck** observatory. If you went up the Hancock in the daytime, try the Sears at night for a great view of the Hancock.

Lake Shore Drive: A trip along the Outer Lake Shore Drive expressway is a delightful way to see the lakefront skyline. On the South Side, you drive from Jackson Park past the sailboats moored in Chicago Harbor at Grant Park, up around Oak Street Beach, to Lincoln Park on the North Side and the boats of Belmont Harbor.

Lincoln Park is worth a separate visit for its **zoo**. It has a terrific ape house, but better than all the usual tropical exotica (of which there's a good sample) is the charming idea of presenting farm animals – pigs, cows, goats, ducks, and chickens – for city kids who never saw a chicken that wasn't fried or barbecued and know little else besides cats, dogs, and pigeons. Similarly, the **Lincoln Park Conservatory** not only has a beautiful orchid col-

Detroit's Rennaisance Center

lection and amazing African and South American trees, but also the simple enchantment of hollyhocks, hyacinths, snapdragons, and daisies in Grandmother's Garden.

Museums in Chicago

Museum Point in Grant Park (1300 South Lake Shore Drive) combines three fascinating exhibitions. The **Shedd Aquarium** (open until 10pm in summer months), is the largest in the world. It has 7,500 species of fish, including a gorgeous Coral Reef collection of 350 Caribbean creatures. If you're lucky, you'll be there when scuba divers go down to feed the big fish. The **Field Museum of Natural History** also encourages visitors to 'play' with some of the exhibits, though you may be intimidated at first by the giant rogue elephants fighting in the main hall. The **Adler Planetarium** offers attractive multimedia sky shows. Apart from the well-presented but by now quite usual exhibits about space exploration, a highlight is the display of astronomical instruments dating back to the times when people still believed the earth was flat. The **Museum of Science and Industry** (South Lake Shore Drive and 57th Street) is the city's most popular museum because you don't just stand there and look, you get into the exhibits and do things. Go down a coal mine, walk through a 16-ft (5-m) high model of the human heart, creep around a captured World War II German submarine, and press buttons and pull all kinds of levers with scarcely a 'Don't Touch' sign in sight.

The **Museum of Surgical Sciences** (1524 North Lake Shore Drive) is the place for those with a sense of the macabre. Inspect the 18th-century amputation devices and antique artificial limbs, but also a reassuring apothecary shop charmingly reconstituted from 1873.

The **Art Institute of Chicago** (Michigan Avenue and Adams Street), at first an art school, now ranks as one of the great American museums. In less than a century it has acquired a collection highlighted by a magnificent range of French Impressionist, Post-Impressionist, and the other major 20th-century art movements.

> A master of the quotable aphorism, Henry Ford said, 'You can buy my cars in any color you like, as long as it's black.'

Detriot (MICHIGAN)

Much older than Chicago, Detroit was established in 1701 by French aristocrat Antoine de la Mothe Cadillac, whose name is now attached to the aristocrat of General Motors' cars. Detroit became the American capital of car manufacturing after Henry Ford built his first motor-driven vehicle in 1892. He revolutionized the American way of life in 1908 with his mass-produced 'Model T,' which made cars available to everyone.

The centerpiece of the **Renaissance Center** (Jefferson and Brush streets), in the dramatic group of five shining black-steel and tinted-glass towers, is the 73-story, cylindrical **Westin Hotel**. The vast lobby has an indoor 'lake' surrounded by trees, and the lounges are reached by ramps and spiral staircases. There are bars and a revolving restaurant on the 73rd floor to view the city – and over the border to Canada.

Civic Center continues the Downtown bustle outdoors around **Hart Plaza**, which contains a striking Noguchi fountain. Jefferson Street goes past the **Ford Auditorium** where the Detroit Symphony Orchestra gives its winter concerts.

The **Cultural Center** (around Woodward and Kirby avenues) brings the city's museums together. The **Detroit Institute of Arts** has some fine Old Masters, including Pieter

Brueghel's *Wedding Dance*, but the most provocative works are the frescoes of Mexican Marxist painter Diego Rivera in Detroit automobile plants, as an epitome of industrial America. The **International Institute** (111 East Kirby) assembles under one roof the cultural artifacts, folklore, costumes, and dolls of 50 different countries.

To escape the city for a while, just take MacArthur Bridge at the end of Jefferson Avenue over to **Belle Isle**, a lovely island park in the Detroit River. You can play tennis or golf here and attend free open-air concerts by the Detroit Concert Band at the Remick Music Shell. For the children, there's a zoo reserved for baby animals; the **Dossin Great Lakes Museum** has a particularly fine exhibition of model ships.

The red, red rocks of the Rocky Mountain states

THE ROCKIES

The Rockies are a series of mountain ranges extending all the way from Mexico to the Canadian Arctic, running along the great Continental Divide that forms the backbone of America. In Montana, Wyoming, Utah, and Colorado they bring the traveler face-to-face with the inspiring natural beauties of America's backcountry, its vast forests and torrents, delightful alpine meadows in summer and wonderful ski slopes in winter.

Formidable barrier to the 19th-century pioneers' westward trek beyond the Great Plains, the Rockies also proved to be a source of great mineral wealth – gold, silver, copper, and, today, uranium.

It was appropriate that the first natural region to receive the federally protected status of 'National Park' (in 1872) should be Yellowstone, the mountain plateau 8,000ft (2,500m) up in the Rockies. To the southeast, Denver is established as the most important city to have grown out of the Rockies' old mining towns and provides the ideal starting point for exploring Colorado's mountain beauty. On the west of the Continental Divide the Mormons established Salt Lake City, originally with the hope that the barrier of the Rockies would protect them from the intolerance of non-believers.

Yellowstone National Park (WYOMING)

Yellowstone is more than a vast landscape of mountains, valleys, rivers, and forests – both living and petrified. It's a perpetual spectacle of exuberant geysers (including star performer Old Faithful) shooting hundreds of feet into the air, volcanic mudpots exploding, hot springs bubbling out of the earth, and waterfalls so high they make Niagara look like an overflowing bathtub. All of this is set against a backdrop of colors that begin with the yellow of the canyon rock that gives the park its name.

The headquarters for the park are at **Mammoth Hot Springs** on the north side of Yellowstone. Visitors should, if possible, come through the north entrance at Gardiner (Montana Highway 89) or make their way up to Mammoth from the West Yellowstone entrance. The information center provides important tips about campgrounds as well as park regulations, trail maps, and a museum of the region's flora, fauna, and geological phenomena.

One of the great geological phenomena of the park is at Mammoth: the lovely silver travertine shelves of a **terrace mountain** being created daily before your eyes. Volcanically heated springs are thrusting up mineral-laden water from underground limestone beds and laying their deposits in terraced pools that form at least a couple of tons of new travertine each day.

Drive 21 miles (34km) south of Mammoth to the Norris junction on the 142-mile (230-km) **Grand Loop** road that will take you around the major landmarks. An interpretive center at the junction points out short hikes (on boardwalks) across the steaming **Norris Geyser Basin**, and provides good explanations of the workings of geysers and hot springs.

With exceptional luck, you may even witness the world's biggest active geyser, the Steamboat. But unlike that of steady, reliable Old Faithful a little farther down the road, its performance is almost as erratic as a volcano. The spouts vary unpredictably from every few days to just once a year. When it does blow, though, it shoots water, steam, rocks, and mud as high as 400ft (122m) into the air.

Farther south, at Madison Junction, the Loop meets the road from the West Yellowstone entrance and curves down along the Firehole River. This well-named river is fed by hot

Mammoth Hot Springs

springs and in places feels like a bath, compared with the plateau streams' chilly 39°F (4°C).

Old Faithful, the most famous site in the park, is 16 miles (26km) south of Madison Junction. This is the geyser that you can rely on to blow every 65 minutes or so. Some geysers in the park are larger, but none is as dependable as Old Faithful, which erupts the most frequently of them all. Another Visitors Center nearby has excellent audiovisual exhibits to explain the phenomenon. This is also the region of three of the park's most active geyser basins, named simply Upper, Midway, and Lower. Be on the lookout, too, for some intriguing, smelly mudpots. These vats of hot, soupy clay are activated by a steam vent, or fumarole.

To escape the crowds that gather at Old Faithful, take the Loop east over to West Thumb (junction with the southern park entrance road, the John D. Rockefeller Memorial Highway) on the shore of beautiful **Yellowstone Lake**. Within strict limitations, you are allowed to fish for cut-throat trout, averaging 18 in (46cm). Boats and tackle can be rented either at Grant Village on the lake's southwest tip or at Fishing Bridge on the north shore. Don't forget that you're competing for the fish with otters, osprey, hawks, and grizzly bears, as well as with coyotes hanging around for what others drop.

From the lake's north shore, the Loop follows the Yellowstone River down to the **Grand Canyon of the Yellowstone**. Approaching from the south, you catch a first sight of the cascading waters of the 109-ft (33-m) Upper Falls. Park a little farther on near the short trail that will take you to **Inspiration Point**, where you can survey the even more dramatic 308-ft (94-m) **Lower Falls** and a panorama of the winding 24-mile (40-km) long canyon. It drops 1,200 to 4,000ft (360 to 1,200m) to the banks of the Yellowstone River. The canyon walls are impregnated with arsenic sulfides that produce every shade and variation of yellow, wonderfully enhanced by the brilliant greens of the surrounding lodgepole-pine forests.

At the northern end of the canyon is **Tower Fall** (near the junction with the northeast park entrance road from Cooke

Yellowstone Facts

Most of Yellowstone's 3,472-sq. mile (8,992-sq. km) expanse is in Wyoming, but it also spills over into Montana to the north and Idaho to the west. Only one of the park's entrances, Gardiner, remains open year-round; the others close between November and May. In winter, the park is snowbound and access is only with a rented snowmobile or in the park's own snowbus. Both Salt Lake City and Denver have local airline services to Yellowstone's airport, where you can rent a car. Though all of the major sights can be reached by car, plan on some good walking too.

Hotels, mostly comfortable but simple cabins, must be reserved well in advance, particularly in winter when only a few are open. Contact TW Services, Yellowstone National Park, WY 82190, tel: (307) 344-7311 (for information: Superintendent, Yellowstone National Park, WY 82190, tel: 307-344-738; <www.nps.gov/yel>).

City). On a sunny day at noon you'll almost certainly see a double rainbow across the 132-ft (40-m) high falls. And if you think that the huge perched boulder is about to tumble down, 'discoverers' of the Tower Fall on August 27, 1870, placed bets that it would be gone by the following day.

East of Tower Junction, off the Lamar Valley Road, lies a fascinating **petrified forest**.

Yellowstone residents

These solid trees, still upright after millions of years, include sycamores, magnolias, maples, oaks, redwoods, walnuts, and willows – their markings still visible. This suggests that Yellowstone was once a great deal warmer than it is today. The forest was covered by volcanic ash rich in silica with which groundwater impregnated the trees and plants, eventually turning them to stone.

Denver (COLORADO)

If you don't believe Denver was once the mining capital of Colorado, look at the 24-carat gold leaf dome on its Capitol Building, or at the local branch of the US Mint that handles one quarter of the nation's gold supplies. The Wild West days have long gone, but locals still like to sport a Stetson hat and checked shirt, for old times' sake. This is the mile-high town, but the air here is unfortunately as polluted as in many other major American cities, and the architecture is relentlessly modern, apart from one colorfully preserved street from the old mining days. But what counts is what you see almost on the city's doorstep – the marvelous backdrop of the Rocky Mountains, Denver's backyard.

The **US Mint** (on Colfax) gives free weekday tours of its money-making plant. You can see gold bullion and the counting-room, full of the finished product. Also on Colfax is the august **Capitol Building** (East 14th and East Colfax streets).

Take the west staircase and stand on the 18th step – that's exactly one mile above sea level.

The best of the modern city is the **Denver Art Museum** (West 14th Avenue and Bannock Street). Its seven-story walls are covered with a million glass tiles over a surface broken up higgledy-piggledy with slotted windows, a true architectural spectacle. The museum contains a first-class collection of Native-American art – totem poles, costumes, and rugs – as well as eight changing exhibitions from all areas of world art.

Old Denver is over on **Larimer Street**, which has conserved its Victorian buildings as art galleries, stores, and cafés – some good Mexican restaurants, too. Larimer Square is done up with courtyards and arcades lit by gas lanterns. But the most authentic piece of old Denver is to be found in the grand lobby of the 1892 **Brown Palace Hotel** (17th and Tremont Place), genteel forerunner of the skylit atrium style of today's glass-tower hotels.

From September to May, the Denver Symphony Orchestra plays at **Boettcher Concert Hall** (14th and Curtis streets), an acoustically sophisticated auditorium-in-the-round which, with the audience encircling the performers, provides a unique

---

Natural Behavior

Human beings are only guests in America's national wilderness areas, and it is not a good idea to interfere with the residents – the moose, antelope, bighorn sheep, bear, bison, fish, and birds. Under no circumstances should you feed bears. The ferocious grizzlies number about 250 in Yellowstone alone, the black bears about 600. A program to remove the bears from the busiest tourist areas has reduced bear-related injuries, but bears still seek out campgrounds for food.

After being reduced by wanton slaughter in the 19th century from millions to just a few hundred on the whole continent, bison are back in the Rocky Mountain area. National parks' ecological policy of strict non-interference with nature means, for instance, that no attempt is made to save the moose herds from starvation in the bitter winters.

opportunity to see the conductor's facial expressions. Classical and popular music concerts are held 16 miles (26km) southwest of town in the open-air arena of **Red Rocks**, set in the middle of red-sandstone outcrops.

If you don't have time for an extended tour of the Rockies, you can still get a taste of one of the higher mountains by driving all the way to the top. Just west of Denver, **Mt Evans** is 14,260ft (4,346m) high, with a paved road to its peak. (Drive 35 miles/57km on Interstate 70 to Idaho Springs and then south on Route 103 to Route 5.)

Gardens galore in Denver

West Central Colorado

An ambitious tour of the major resorts of west-central Colorado will take you on a beautiful 360-mile (583-km) circuit through the Rocky Mountains, but if time is limited you may prefer to aim for just one of the big three:

Aspen: Aspen is the best-known resort town in the state. At 7,937ft (2,419m) it provides wonderful winter-sports opportunities, but it's also a delight in summer, both for its music festival and for the hiking, camping, fishing, and horseback riding in the surrounding **White River National Forest**. In the 1880s the town made its fortune from silvermining, but the market collapsed in 1893 and the town was deserted until revived as a sports and cultural center after World War II. Some of the old Victorian buildings have been preserved with considerable charm and taste, particularly the Opera House and the lovely Hotel Jerome.

A stroll in Rocky Mountain National Park

The Aspen Music Festival in summer presents opera, classical music, and jazz of the highest order. International stars like to hang out here. They take advantage of the easygoing atmosphere in the Downtown mall of stores and outdoor cafés or excursions into the spectacular **Maroon Bells** mountains southwest of town. In winter, skiing opportunities vary from the family slopes on Buttermilk and nearby Snowmass to the challenges on Aspen Highlands or the famous Ruthie's Run on Aspen Mountain.

Vail: North of the White River National Forest, this is a very successful modern ski-resort with Swiss-style chalets. In summer it caters to tennis and golf enthusiasts – the only real problem with the golf course being that the scenery is so spectacular it can easily distract you from your game. Surprisingly, there is also enough gentle landscape around to make bicycling a special pleasure. Anglers fish for excellent trout in Gore Creek and Eagle River.

Glenwood Springs: This destination offers the luxury of a 405-ft (123.5-m) long swimming pool fed by a stream of natural warm water to a temperature of 85–90°F (29–32°C). The waters were much prized by Native Americans as energizers before going on the hunt or warpath. They'll definitely relax you after some exhilarating rafting down the **Colorado River**.

Salt Lake City (UTAH)

A unique phenomenon in American life, Salt Lake City is a community founded and sustained on theological doctrine – that of the Mormons, or, to give them their full name, the Church of Jesus Christ of Latter-day Saints. It also manages to be an agreeable town of friendly (and not only Mormon) people, with bright shopping centers and outdoor cafés as well as impressive monuments to an historic spirit of adventure and courage.

All this is carved out of a desert of salt flats that stretches from the foot of the Wasatch Range of the Rockies around the Great Salt Lake all the way across Utah to the mountains of Nevada. This geographical isolation has motivated the people of Salt Lake City to keep up a busy cultural life of ballet, choral music, and art exhibitions.

Temple Square is the all-important center of Salt Lake City, a 10-acre (4-hectare) compound surrounded by a 15-ft (4.5-m) high wall containing the nucleus of the Mormons' church buildings, including the Temple, Tabernacle, and Visitors Center. The solid granite Temple, 40 years in the building, is closed to non-believers, but the celebrated **Tabernacle** is open to everyone. Its vast 250-ft (76-m) long and 150-ft (46-m) wide turtleback dome, originally made of wood shingles but now encased in aluminium, was constructed only with wooden dowels, no nails, since iron was too scarce in Utah in the 1860s. The dome stands on 44 sandstone pillars at its periphery and provides wonderful acoustics for the great Mormon Tabernacle Choir. The 375 singers hold free rehearsals on Thursday evenings. A monumental 11,623-pipe organ enhances the rather stark interior of the Tabernacle (there are free organ recitals daily at noon).

Beehive House (67 East South Temple) was built in 1854 as the residence of Brigham Young when he served as President of the LDS church and Governor of the Utah Territory. It is now

Salt Lake City's stunning natural setting

a museum. Rooms, decorated with period furnishings, include the playroom, the fairy castle, and the gracious sitting room, where each evening the Young family sang and prayed together. The life of the early community is portrayed in the **Pioneer Museum** (300 North Main Street). The **State Capitol**, a copper-domed, Corinthian-style building of Utah granite and marble, affords a sensational view of the Wasatch Mountains.

The ZCMI (Zion Co-operative Mercantile Institution) at 15 South Main was one of the country's first department stores, built in 1868. Now its charming, ornate cast-iron facade with slender Corinthian columns serves as the front of a bustling shopping mall with attractive boutiques, art galleries, and gift shops. Similarly, **Trolley Square** (5th South and 7th East streets) has converted old trolley barns for new uses; now they house restaurants, stores, and a theater. Monday night – the Mormons' Family Evening – is a popular time to visit the ice-cream parlors and movie houses.

Just south of the square, **Liberty Park** makes a lovely picnic ground, with arbors, a swimming pool, a boating lake, an amusement park, and the popular Tracy Aviary. Concerts and festivals are held here in the summer. The **Salt Palace Auditorium** is another venue for concerts and events; on the same grounds, the **Bicentennial Arts Center** is the venue for performances of theater, the ballet, and the music of the Utah Symphony Orchestra, with art exhibitions.

You shouldn't leave without a vist to the **Great Salt Lake**. Even if you prefer not to float in its hot, sticky, 25 percent saline water, the sight alone is worth the diversion. The lake, surrounded by marshland and salt flats, is indeed an impressive sight, but much more refreshing is **Wasatch National Forest**, a haven of peace and a pleasure. Opportunities are here for hiking, camping, trout fishing, or autumn hunting for deer, moose, antelope, and elk. The area is also a popular destination for winter sports such as skiing and snowboarding, and was the site for the Winter Olympics of 2002.

Mormons

The Mormons' founder, New Englander Joseph Smith, began and ended his religious career with divine revelations. The first, in the 1820s, was that the Native Americans were the Lost Tribes of Israel to be redeemed from paganism by Smith and his followers. Twenty years later, with 15,000 converts in Nauvoo, Illinois, he was directed by revelation to follow the path of polygamy, since the prophet Isaiah had said in the Bible that 'seven women shall take hold of one man.' Smith in fact took 27 wives, and others followed suit until a conflict with dissidents ended in his lynching. Brigham Young succeeded as the Mormons' Prophet, inheriting five of Smith's widows to add to a dozen of his own wives, and led his people on an arduous 1,000-mile (1,690-km) trek across the prairies, Great Plains, and the Rocky Mountains to a new promised land. 'This is the place' were his much-quoted words on surveying the dry expanses of Utah's salt flats. Polygamy remained the official practice until the United States made its disavowal the condition of Utah statehood in 1896.

**The Alamo, symbol of the
Southwest's Texas**

THE SOUTHWEST

The region *par excellence* of America's wide open spaces, the Southwest stretches across most of the much touted American 'Sun Belt.' It covers the vast ranchlands and oil country of Texas, the rugged highlands of New Mexico first settled by the Indians and Spanish conquistadors, and Arizona's deserts rising to pine-forested mountains. Their culmination is the nation's most awe-inspiring sight, a phenomenon that humbles the most blasé of world travelers – the Grand Canyon.

Perhaps it's the sheer majesty of these open spaces that sustains in the people of this region that particular brand of American individualism and independent spirit that has been a little tamed in the cities of the rest of the country. This makes Southwesterners perhaps less accessible to outsiders at first, but if you take the trouble to win their confidence, you'll find the most cordial, cheerful, and colorful company in the country.

Don't even consider visiting Texas, New Mexico, and Arizona without a car. While buses and planes will take you from town to town, the distances around the towns and between the sights are more than shoe leather or local bus services were meant to deal with. Choose your season well: spring and summer bring the great dry heat of the desert or the humidity and high temperatures of towns like Houston. The region was settled by hardy pioneers, and you must come to it with some of the same spirit.

Texas is an acquired taste. The endless cattle ranges, and the sparkling prosperity of the skyscrapers in Dallas and Houston are insistently impressive. But in the end, the name Texas evokes not only a geographical location but people with a special attitude to life, and this is what is hard to grasp. The pushy arrogance and braggadocio have become legendary, to a point where Texans who might by nature – just a few of them – be shy, retiring folk feel obliged to live up to the image. Texas is no longer the largest state in the US, that honor having gone to Alaska when it joined the union in 1959, but the self-image as the biggest and the best remains. Houston and Dallas show the modern form this Texan self-confidence has taken, and San Antonio shows the historic background from which it has come.

Part of the joy of New Mexico is the predominance of a completely different architecture from that of the rest of the country. Adobe (dried mud) houses with tranquil courtyards, arcaded plazas, and fountains give a welcome illusion of coolness in the summer. You won't find them everywhere, but there are enough to forget for a while the rectangular blocks of skyscraper-land. Another pleasure here is the desert landscape and the glowing pink-and-gold light that gives its aridity a jewel-like quality, an excellent ambiance for meditation. It's not surprising that the state attracted so many artists, flower children, and hippies in the 1960s.

After the skyscrapers of New York City, the rugged desert and mountain landscapes of Arizona are the most likely component of the world's image of America. For history and Hollywood, this is as far as the Far West gets. The Hopi Indians settled here in what was Europe's Middle Ages and the Navajo followed. In the 19th century, the cattle and sheep ranchers fought for control of the plains and battled with Apache heroes Cochise and Geronimo. Copper, gold, silver, uranium, and other ores made the state rich, and the year-round sun has since warmed the hearts of retired colonists from the cold Midwest. For the visitor, Arizona offers the matchless wonder of the Grand Canyon, the awe of the deserts, and the mirage-like towers of the city of Phoenix.

Dallas (TEXAS)

Television, movies, and the national tragedy of John F. Kennedy's assassination have made this one of the best-known cities in America. The skyline looming out of the plain says it all. A forest of towers sheathed in silver or bronze mirror-glass reflect the dawn as more golden, the noon's blue sky more blue, the rosy sunset blood red. The most attractive skyscrapers are the glassy Allied Bank Tower and the gleaming slabs of the Hyatt Regency Hotel. They stand beside **Reunion Tower** (300 Reunion Boulevard, off the Stemmons Freeway). The tower has a revolving cocktail lounge, restaurant, and observation deck for a fine view of the Texas infinity.

Dallas dazzles after dusk

The **John Fitzgerald Kennedy Memorial** (Main and Market) is a stark and eloquent monument to the shooting of the president on November 22, 1963. The 30-ft (9-m) high walls enclose a broken square that is approached along a gently sloping ramp, a space for meditation. The assassination is understandably something the people of Dallas would rather forget, but visitors just won't let them.

Due to public demand, the former Texas Book Depository nearby, from which Lee Harvey Oswald was said to have fired the fatal shots from the sixth floor, has been turned into the **Sixth Floor Museum** (tel: 214-653-6666; open daily). The museum houses exhibits about J.F.K.'s campaign, his social and economic programs, and the space race. Cameras used by spectators watching the motorcade can be seen, as well as the famous Zapruder camera and some of the footage it recorded of the assassination, the best visual documentation to have surfaced. A videotape of the dramatic events of the day includes a tearful Walter Cronkite (America's most respected newscaster) announcing the President's death.

West of the J.F.K. Memorial is the little **Log Cabin** (Market and Elm), a replica of the one pioneer John Neely Bryan built in 1841 when he came to settle in this part of Texas, the site of the future city of Dallas. The tiny cabin, which was brought here, perhaps as a cheerful antidote to the assassination monument, served both as post office and courthouse.

This resolutely forward-looking town has preserved just one area in which it has assembled the remnants of its past – **Old City Park** (Gano and St Paul streets). Here you can picnic on the grass among restored Victorian houses, old log cabins, an 1886 railroad depot, a bandstand, turn-of-the-20th-century stores, and a Greek Revival mansion from 1855.

But otherwise, it's the people rather than the buildings that carry the past with them in this town. See them at their best at the **Farmer's Market** (1010 South Pearl), a collection of ramshackle tin-roofed stands where they sell Texas-size fruit and vegetables, chew tobacco, spit, or pick a mean guitar – good ol' boys to a man.

One of the more interesting local monuments is **Neiman-Marcus** (Main and Ervay), the legendary department store. Nothing is too outrageous for them to sell – solid gold bathroom fittings, pet lion cubs or even His-and-Hers jet aircraft. Neiman-Marcus stores are now located all over America, but these temples to conspicuous consumption started in Texas, of course.

The free **Dallas Museum of Art** (tel: 214-922-1200; open daily) is a showcase of treasures money can't buy. But you can view the collection, particularly strong in 19th- and 20th-century art, housed in a landmark building purpose-designed by Edward Barnes.

In the middle of the formidable fanfare of downtown Dallas, you can easily retreat for a moment's tranquillity in the lovely triangle of **Thanksgiving Square**, a peaceful little oasis of immaculate lawns, gardens, trees, and channels of water, with a bridge leading to a spiral chapel. In the square is one of the entrances to **Underground City** – 3 miles (5km) of subterranean stores and restaurants.

Houston *(TEXAS)*

Houston is oil and space. It's a hot, humid town that has burgeoned into one of the most prosperous business communities in America (though there are some sections of the city that are still struggling). To deal with the heat and humidity, there is an underground network of air-conditioned concourses (fuelled by local oil) that link the downtown skyscrapers.

Oil is proclaimed on its skyline by the striking black wedge-shaped towers of **Pennzoil Plaza**, designed by Philip Johnson, and the gabled, red-granite Republic Bank Center. You can see how the black gold is drawn from the earth at the **Museum of Natural Science** (1 Hermann Circle Drive at Hermann Park). The displays of drilling and refining technology include a model of an offshore oil rig.

Texas Longhorns, the time tested breed for serious ranchers

The **Museum of Fine Arts** (1001 Bissonnet, tel: 713-639-7300; open Tues–Sun) has collections of Indian and pre-Columbian art, while the contemporary art section is a constant source of surprise as wealthy donors bring back new treasures. For local color, the most exciting works on display are the studies of cowboy life by painter and sculptor Frederic Remington. His are the images that have made bucking broncos and gunfighters the icons of the Wild West.

The **Rothko Chapel** (3900 Yupon Street) is a lovely – if somewhat austere – non-denominational place of worship, housing the

Downtown Houston; it's new, it's shiny, and it's big

starkly contemplative purple-and-black canvases of Mark Rothko. The chapel and neighboring **Menil Collection** of art – strong on the Surrealists and on primitive and Asian work – was given to Houston by philanthropists Jean and Dominique de Menil.

About 25 miles (40km) southeast of Houston on Interstate 45, then NASA Road, is the **Lyndon B. Johnson Space Center** (tel: 800-972-0369). This is the controlling hub of the United States space program, where astronauts train and NASA has its monitoring center for manned space flights. The Visitor Orientation Center is a splendid museum of space equipment, rockets, lunar modules, space capsules, and moon rock. Guided tours around the Mission Control Center are given by knowledgeable cadets, and you can also visit the Skylab Training Room, the living and working quarters of NASA's space laboratory.

San Antonio *(TEXAS)*

For visitors, San Antonio is the most accessible of Texan towns, the historic center of the state's Spanish-Mexican beginnings and delightfully inviting with its River Walk through the heart of Downtown.

The **Alamo** (Alamo Plaza), built as the Spanish Mission San Antonio de Valero in 1718, is the hallowed fortress where 187 Americans fought and succumbed to 5,000 Mexican soldiers under General Santa Ana in 1836. They'd been sent to put down American resistance to Mexico's authoritarian rule of its Texas province. The Americans' heroic stand inspired the revolt which finally won Texas independence and subsequent admission to the US as the Lone Star State.

Today the Alamo is a museum of that momentous battle. Among other memorabilia, it displays the Bowie knife, the curved-bladed weapon fashioned by Colonel James Bowie, joint commander of the Alamo. It was the other commander, William Travis, who issued the order: 'Victory or death.' Best-known of the Alamo heroes was Davy Crockett, who devoted his life to self-promoting acts of courage in Tennessee before being defeated when he stood in a congressional election. He told his constituents 'You can all go to hell, I'm going to Texas,' and there he died.

You can see where the Spanish used to rule Texas at the **Spanish Governor's Palace** (tel: 210-224-0601), a rather grim edifice dating back to 1749, still emblazoned with the Habsburg eagle of Spain's ruling family over the entrance. The house is furnished with pieces from the Spanish and Mexican eras. You can also see the Mexicans' old adobe houses and stone patios in **La Villita**, the residential neighborhood south of the river along Villita Street. For Mexican shopping, a visit to the old market place, El Mercado (515 W. Commerce) is always lively and fun.

Bar Tips

If you want to make friends with Texans in a bar, don't order white wine or fancy cocktails. If you think you can manage it with a straight face and without spluttering, ask the bartender for a 'long neck' (bottled beer) together with a shot of whisky. Don't say 'Scotch,' don't specify rye or bourbon. Just drink the whisky – it'll be bourbon – in one gulp. Smile politely at your neighbor. Ease your way gently into conversation, don't get bumptious or pushy. Don't talk dirty. Or politics. Don't argue the merits of European and American football. Don't even try to explain the rules of soccer. Just ask how good the Dallas Cowboys are this year compared with the past. Don't talk about Houston in Dallas or about Dallas in Houston. But follow these tips and you can't fail to make friends.

The Mission at San Antonio

The river is San Antonio's pride and joy. The **Paseo del Rio**, or **River Walk**, meanders nearly 3 miles (5km) around a horseshoe curve through town. Below the bustle of traffic, you can walk past banana plants and bougainvillaea shading outdoor cafés and ice cream parlors, nightclubs, and craft shops. Water-taxis and river cruises are available at the Market Street Bridge, or dine by candlelight on the pleasure barges. Beyond the river, the water garden of the Paseo del Alamo stretches to the Alamo.

The nicest museum in town is the **Hertzberg Circus Collection** (West Market Street), where working models present a comprehensive history of the circus from its early days in England to the American heyday of the P.T. Barnum era. Clown costumes, Tom Thumb's dwarf carriage, and a complete circus ring make a nostalgic exhibition.

For a panoramic view of San Antonio and the surrounding country go out to **HemisFair Park**, a relic of the 1968 World's Fair, where there's an observatory on the 652-ft (199-m) Tower of the Americas. The park is also the site of the Institute of Texan Cultures, devoted to the folklore of the 26 ethnic groups that together have created the state of Texas.

Mission Road running south of town takes you out to the missions that were the basis of Spanish colonization in the 18th century, with Catholic priests converting Native Americans to Christianity while a garrison of soldiers subdued the recalcitrant and searched for gold. **Mission San José** (5 miles/8km south on

US Highway 281) is the best preserved of these spiritual and military installations. Founded in 1720, this 'Queen of the Missions' has a Spanish baroque entrance. Inside, you can visit the soldiers' spartan quarters, the granary, and natives' workshops.

Santa Fe *(NEW MEXICO)*

Founded by the Spanish in 1610, **Santa Fe** is the oldest capital city in the United States. The atmosphere in the historic center of town, for all the invasion of hotels and souvenir shops, still gives a hint of that more leisurely Spanish and Indian era. The rose-colored adobe structures with their *vigas*, log beams holding up the ceilings and roofs, managing miraculously to be both solid and graceful in form, offer their shady arcades as a delightful shelter from the heat of the day.

The **Plaza** is the focus of old Santa Fe. On its north side is the Palace of the Governors, the oldest public building in the US (1610), now housing part of the **Museum of New Mexico** devoted to the history and prehistory of the state. In the arcade along the facade of the palace, Pueblo Indians sell handmade silver and turquoise jewelry (turquoise of fair quality still comes in considerable quantities from the hills of New Mexico). Navajo and international folk art is displayed in annexes of the museums located along the old Santa Fe Trail.

An old Spanish church in Santa Fe

Canyon Road, running along the south bank of the Santa Fe River, is the sleepy quarter where the painters, sculptors, and craftspeople have their studios and galleries. Walk in and watch them work. The landscape artists tend to be the best, the ambient color and light being such an inspiration. The renowned **Santa Fe Opera** is

Young Native American

housed in a wonderful open-air setting, an amphitheatre carved out of the hillside (partially roofed in the unlikely event of rain) 7 miles (11km) north of town on the road to Taos.

Taos (NEW MEXICO)

In the early 20th century, Taos was an art colony much loved by British novelist D.H. Lawrence. It continues to attract artists and their groupies, who live an easy hand-to-mouth existence just off the town **Plaza**. The town's colorful street life blends society's bohemian element with Taos Indians, Spanish-American farmers, and assorted sightseers. Back in the days of Spanish rule, Taos was the center of the Pueblo Revolt (1680) which ultimately lost New Mexico for the Spanish. North of town, the **Taos Pueblo** is a centuries-old Indian village with 900 residents still inhabiting the sprawling five-story apartment buildings – forerunner of modern America's condominiums. The jewelry, blankets, drums, and baskets sold here make excellent gifts.

At Ranchos de Taos, 4 miles (6.5km) south on Highway 68, the 1772 **San Francisco de Asis Mission** is the most attractive of the adobe churches. A sturdy, buttressed affair, it looks like a massive piece of sculpture.

Phoenix (ARIZONA)

The most spectacular thing about Phoenix is its setting in the **Valley of the Sun**, the perfect backdrop to a Western movie, with the forbidding red Superstition Mountains to the east and towering Camelback Mountain northeast of town.

If passing through Phoenix in the summer, you may find that it's just too hot to get out of your air-conditioned car. However, there are some museums that are worth visiting. The **Heard Museum** (22 East Monte Vista) is one of the best of its kind in the country. It traces the history of Native Americans of the Southwest from the first cave-dwellers and Pueblo Indians – with a wonderful collection of Kachina dolls – to modern times.

The **Pueblo Grande Museum** (4619 East Washington) is an on-site archaeological excavation of a Hohokam Indian settlement believed to date back some 2,000 years. The ruins, spread across a broad mound, mark out a civilization that disappeared around the year 1400. As preparation for the flora you'll see on your desert drive, visit the **Desert Botanical Gardens**, 3 miles (5km) east of Pueblo Grande.

Phoenix might be a good starting point for the Grand Canyon. There are flights directly up to the canyon from here or, if the prospect of a desert drive appeals, then rent a car here.

The Grand Canyon

No picture, no words will ever match the physical reality of the **Grand Canyon**'s beauty. You'll see it and still won't believe it. That moment will come when you approach the **South Rim** of the 277-mile (449-km) long, serpentine canyon. Look down to its 1-mile (1.5-km) deep floor where the once-mighty Colorado River has eroded a passage and millions of years of earth upheavals have gouged out a theater for the performance of the grand geological drama. Plan your trip to the Grand Canyon like a military operation. It's always best to avoid the high season of May to September, if possible. There are camping facilities and hotels on the **North Rim**, but that's really for *habitués*. First-timers should concentrate on the **South Rim**.

Make reservations well in advance if you want to go camping; <www.grand-canyon.national-park.com/camping>. Lodging is also available in **Grand Canyon Village**. Booths at Grand

Grand Canyon Village provide information about the bus tours of the main Rim Drive, bicycling around the rim, hiking or riding mules down to the canyon floor, or rafting along the Colorado River. Hiking and mule-riding are for the hardy who can rise at dawn, face high temperatures at noon, and generally rough it. Rafting is a spectacular way of seeing the canyon and perfectly safe in the hands of experienced guides.

The **Visitors Center** at Grand Canyon Village is a must for initial orientation. The rangers here and at key spots along the Rim Drive provide fascinating information on the geology, flowers, animal life, and anthropological history. Especially interesting are the Indians whose dwellings, built into the canyon cliffs, are still visible today on the North Rim.

Up on the rim are fine **nature trails** through forests of juniper and piñon pine. Every now and again you emerge in a clearing on the edge of the canyon to peer down at the giant mounds or buttes rising like Egyptian pyramids or Aztec temples, and bearing such

One of the wonders of the natural world – the Grand Canyon

names as Zoroaster Temple or Cheops Pyramid. Some of the other rock formations bear such ominously fanciful names as Skeleton Point and the Phantom Ranch.

> **The Grand Canyon was created solely by the erosion of the Colorado River. From the rim of the canyon, the river looks like a stream.**

Shutle buses run along the 8-mile (13-km) **West Rim** (closed to private cars from May to September), stopping off for wonderful views at Hopi Point, Mohave Point, and Pima Point. Other buses pass frequently and might pick up walkers.

You should attempt to hike only if you are fit and well prepared; although distances are small, the terrain is rough and temperatures are extreme. Wear good walking shoes, a sunhat, sunscreen, and protective clothing, and carry plenty of drinking water.

The easiest route is the **Bright Angel Trail**, leaving from Bright Angel Lodge. Start at daybreak, as you can safely count on a good three hours going downhill, and six or seven hours coming back up. The trail zigzags down 1½ miles (2.5km) to a resthouse (you'll find an emergency telephone installed there), another 1½ miles to the Jacob's Ladder Resthouse, still zigzagging and then straightening out to the beautiful **Indian Garden** at Garden Creek. You can stay overnight at this ranger station and campground providing you have a reservation, which should be made at least six months in advance.

Stalwart hikers will continue the next morning along Garden Creek around the self-explanatory **Devil's Corkscrew** down Pipe Creek to the River Resthouse beside the Colorado River. With an advance reservation, hikers can also stay at the bunkhouse-style accommodations at Phantom Ranch. A more challenging hike is the steeper **Kaibab Trail** from the Yaki Point Road east of the village.

The joy of the hikes is that they take you away from the crowd along the Rim Drive, though even here you can always walk a few hundred yards away and enjoy the beauty of this phenomenon in near tranquility.

THE WEST

The West is America's most varied playground, catering to the crazy, the lazy, and the easygoing. Only those in search of the hectic are discouraged: here, nobody rushes. While Las Vegas carries the madness inland to the desert, Seattle on the northwest Pacific Coast introduces a note of sanity in its healthy green state of Washington. But these are the appendages to the American mecca of all dreamers, European and American alike: California. A land blessed with sun and sea and oranges and ice cream, California is quite simply the ultimate fantasy land. It is as far west as man can go without starting to go east. Stand on the beach at Malibu, stare out at the Pacific Ocean or back at the Santa Monica mountains, and everything seems possible: balmy winters, shining summers, snow if you want it.

It's no accident that this is the chosen home of America's film industry. California offers every imaginable landscape – Swiss

Living the dream on the West Coast

Alps, Sahara Desert, English meadows, African jungle – all just a few miles from the freeway. And what isn't already here – a Roman forum or Egyptian pyramid – can be built in a few days with the great wealth that California has amassed in little more than a century. Its prosperity is truly overwhelming and constantly renewed – beginning with the gold of the Sierras, spreading across the great Central Valley to the gigantic combines of agribusiness (mere agriculture was just a passing phase), and on to the coast for oil and the aerospace industry. Californians are perfectly prepared to work, and work hard, but they can't wait to get back to the tennis court or swimming pool, go surfing in the Pacific or hiking in Yosemite National Park.

Gun-slinging sherif

In constant quest of the new, in clothes, music, ideas, toys, and religions, people here cling to their joyously accepted role as America's latest pioneers. Hula hoops, skateboards, windsurfing, roller-discos – it all starts, flourishes, and fizzles out in California, while the rest of the world takes note and – more often than not – follows suit.

Many Californians would like to divide their state into two separate entities: Northern and Southern California – corresponding to two distinct frames of mind represented by San Francisco and Los Angeles respectively. But in fact there's a little bit of both – San Francisco's sophistication and Los Angeles' sunny craziness – all over the state.

This itinerary begins in San Francisco and its nearby wine valleys and works its way down the Pacific coast to Los Angeles and San Diego before taking off for the national parks of

Yosemite, Sequoia, and Death Valley. Whatever routes you choose, if time permits, you should also try to make an excursion to California's favorite out-of-state playground, Las Vegas.

You can get to almost all these places by train or bus, and air travel is relatively inexpensive compared with the rest of the country. However, California is inevitably the land of the car, and it will be difficult to enjoy the full scope of the vast and varied landscape without driving. San Francisco is a town for walking, with buses and cable cars to help you up and down the hills, but Los Angeles is resolutely a drivers' town. Yosemite and Sequoia are wonderful places for hiking.

> **San Francisco is a city of at least a dozen neighborhoods, as distinct and original as the people who live in them.**

San Francisco (CALIFORNIA)

San Franciscans are unashamedly in love with their life. All over the place you see the boast: 'Everybody's Favorite City.' The town's natural setting, the hills around the bay, makes it uncommonly cozy; the zip in the air is invigorating, and even the fog rolling off the ocean is romantic rather than chilling, the mists rolling over Twin Peaks, enveloping the Golden Gate Bridge or blanketing Golden Gate Park are sights not to be missed. The enthusiasm of the residents is difficult to resist, and easy to understand.

If you have a car, the best way to begin is by taking the **49-Mile Scenic Drive**, an 80-km comprehensive tour that gives an overall picture before you explore in detail. Stop off at **Twin Peaks**, south of Golden Gate Park, for a panoramic view of the city and its bay. Then put away the car and use the city's first-class public transportation, combined with a pair of good walking shoes. The city is great to explore on foot, but be warned: the hills are every bit as steep as they look.

Start at the bridge. There is more than one, but *the* bridge is of course the **Golden Gate Bridge**. Named 'Golden Gate' for the channel it crosses, between San Francisco and Marin County, the bridge itself is colored a deep burned sienna or reddish-brown, depending on the light. At 4,200ft (1,280m), this masterpiece by engineer Joseph Strauss is not the longest, but many agree that it's the most beautiful suspension bridge in the world. Completed in 1937, it took four years to build and takes four years to repaint – a job that begins again as soon as it's finished. Walking among the joggers and bicyclists over the swaying bridge with its rattling lamposts is as exciting an adventure as climbing the Eiffel Tower in Paris.

While you're here, spare a thought for **Oakland Bay Bridge** just visible in the distance. The silvery bridge swings across to Berkeley and Oakland via Yerba Buena island, and at 8¼ miles/13.5km is one of the world's longest.

South of the Golden Gate Bridge is the **Presidio**, site of the original garrison built by the Spanish to protect their settlement in 1776. It was the headquarters of the Sixth Army – remarkably green and pretty for a military establishment.

The Golden Gate Bridge connects the city with Marin County

Historic ship at Hyde Street Pier, Fisherman's Wharf

Take in a manificent view of the Golden Gate from Lincoln Park at 34th Avenue and Clement, the site of the **California Palace of the Legion of Honor** (tel: 415-750-3600; open Tues–Sun), which was built as a memorial to the state's World War I casualties. An exact replica of the Legion of Honor Palace in Paris, the neoclassical building is now one of the city's major art museums, housing important collections of ancient art, European decorative art, painting, sculpture, and works on paper. One of the world's finest collections of Rodin's sculptures can be found here; at the entrance is one of the five existing bronze casts of his *The Thinker*.

On the way down to the Yacht Harbor is the **Palace of Fine Arts**, dating from the 1915 Panama-Pacific Exposition. The exterior, a hodgepodge of classical architecture and reinforced-concrete evoking a Roman ruin, contrasts with the modern technological wizardry of the **Exploratorium** (3601 Lyon Street, tel: (415) 563-7337) inside. The museum's holography, lasers, and solar-operated musical instruments are great for the kids on a rainy day.

From the western Yacht Harbor make your way along Marina Boulevard, past pretty waterfront houses, to busy and bustling **Fisherman's Wharf**. Stroll around, look at the boats, and nibble shrimp or crab from the seafood stands along the wharf. It's also a major center for the revival of street theater and music. Check out the stores and restaurants of **Ghirardelli Square**, a converted red-brick chocolate factory, and **The Cannery**, once a fruit-processing plant. Directly east of Fisherman's Wharf is popular **Pier 39**, another complex of shops, restaurants, and entertainments. Visitors are rewarded with spectacular views of the bay, Alcatraz, and the Golden Gate Bridge.

The Hills: There are 40 hills, and they are San Francisco's pride. A tour of Nob Hill (Powell or California street cable car), Telegraph Hill (bus), and Russian Hill (cable car) will give you a good sense of the past and present splendors of San Francisco's wealthy residents.

The imposing Victorian houses of **Nob Hill**, where the 'nobs,' or nabobs, lived, were wiped out in the 1906 earthquake – with one notable exception: the impressive brownstone house of James Flood, now the highly exclusive Pacific Union Club. You can't get in, but you can loiter (with appropriate decorum) in the hill's two landmark hotels – the Fairmont and the Mark Hopkins. Each has a panoramic bar; the stiff price of a drink in either one of them is worth it for the view, easpecially at sunset, and the bartenders do know how to shake a cocktail.

One of the best reasons for climbing **Telegraph Hill** is to reach the breathtaking view from the top of **Coit Tower**. Built with a bequest from a local widow in 1934 to honor the city's fire department, it is designed to recall the nozzle of a fire hose.

Cable Capers

A delightful way of riding San Francisco's hills is aboard the fabled cable cars. It's the most enjoyable ride in town, especially hanging on the outside step – dangerous but legal – as the Powell Street car clangs up and down Nob Hill, views passing in slow, bumpy motion.

The cars were first installed in 1873, and one of the originals is in the Cable Car Museum, which is also the system's working center, at Washington and Mason streets. The handmade cars are constantly refurbished and overhauled, so don't be surprised if a line is not in service. Riders are not allowed on with ice cream, because the bone-shaking ride would likely land it in the lap of a fellow passenger.

Coit Tower and the Transamerica Pyramid, San Francisco

Russian Hill may be less opulent than the other two hills, but its gardens and immaculate little cottages make it the most appealing. It's name came from the Russian enclave that made it's home here. The constant ups and downs of the city's streets reach a crazy climax on **Lombard Street**, between Hyde and Leavenworth. After you negotiate the incredibly serpentine plunge, weaving in and out of the seven sudden bends, you wont quibble about its claim to be the 'crookedest street in the world.'

North Beach: In spite of its name, North Beach can lay no claim to being a beach at all. It's the district north of the Broadway and Columbus intersection that is both center of the Italian community and focus of the city's artistic and intellectual life. Part of it used to be known as the 'Barbary Coast,' an infamous den of iniquity where sailors came for the brothels, while their captains shanghaied drunken or otherwise unconscious civilians for their crews.

Since the 1950s, when poet Lawrence Ferlinghetti gathered his fellow beatniks around his City Lights Bookshop, North

Beach has been the place where California's new ideas, intellectual and other, are first tried out. The more literate of the hippies in the 1960s congregated here rather than the more hedonistic enclaves of Haight-Ashbury. In the 1970s it was the turn of the 'mellows,' the smiling younger brothers and sisters of the hippies, gliding around on quiet roller skates, eating frozen yogurt, and espousing the newly-emerging ecological causes.

Chinese newcomers are making inroads into the Asian and Italian neighborhood, clustered around Columbus, Stockton, Vallejo, and Green streets. There are many Asian and Italian grocery stores, pastry shops, espresso bars, cafés, and restaurants. But the seedy tradition of the Barbary Coast lives on in the (shrinking) number of 'topless' joints on Broadway.

Chinatown: This expansive neighborhood has evolved from a ghetto imposed on the Chinese in the 19th century by the founders of the city into a proud, self-assertive community. Gone are the days of the Tong wars to establish control of the community's underworld and opium dens. The vicarious thrill that these adventures provided has been replaced by a general civic pride, although Chinatown's elders are now begining to show some concern for the future. Rising rents have been driving out family

businesses, and the upwardly mobile have continued their exodus to the suburbs. More than 100,000 Chinese live in San Francisco, making it the largest Chinese community outside Asia. The week-long Chinese New Year celebrations in February are a major event for much of the city.

The main neighborhood is bounded by Broadway, Bush, Kearny, and Stockton, with eight blocks of Grant Avenue

Chinatown

as its colorful axis. An ornamental arch at the Bush Street end of Grant marks the south entry to Chinatown. Flanking it are two houses of Chinese design. Beyond the arch, life is more resolutely Chinese, and hearing English is more the exception than the norm.

On a smaller scale, but with the same cultural pride, is **Japan Town** – J-town to San Franciscans. Its Cultural and Trade Center at Geary between Laguna and Fillmore streets includes schools of cookery and Japanese flower arrangement, a Japanese theater, and a hotel with Japanese amenities – sunken baths, mattresses on tatami mats, kimonoed maids, and indoor rock gardens.

Civic Center: After leaving the exotic trappings of the East, you may want to remind yourself of America's predominant mainstream culture, the Anglo-Saxon variety. In the wedge formed by Market Street, the city's main thoroughfare, and Van Ness Street, is a sprawling complex of municipal, state, and federal buildings, recently cleaned and refurbished, and known collectively as the Civic Center.

It was initiated in an ambitious burst of city planning after the 1906 earthquake, and the early structures are in Renaissance style. As well as the City Hall

City Hall, part of the Civic Center

and Main Public Library, the complex includes the Veterans' Building, the Opera House, where the United Nations Charter was first signed in 1945, the Asian Art Museum, and the Symphony Hall.

Union Square: For a shopping detour, go down Market Street and turn off at Powell. Union Square is the place to go for fashionable boutiques, specialty stores, flower stands, and large department stores. Continue on to Montgomery Street, the heart of San Francisco's wealthy Financial District. You're not likely to miss the **Transamerica Pyramid**, an 853-ft (260-m) spike at the corner of Montgomery and Washington streets.

SoMa: For a cultural detour, head across Market Street to the area called SoMa (**South of Market.**) **Yerba Buena Gardens** is an arts and entertainment complex interspersed with tranquil patches of greenery that occupies the entire block between 3rd and 4th streets. The complex overlooks the **Esplanade**, a

SoMa's got the MOMA – and the Yerba Buena Gardens, too.

pretty downtown park. Adjacent to the Esplanade is a four-story entertainment complex sponsored by Sony, the **Metreon**, where big-screen movie theaters and technology feature prominently. International touring shows tend to roost at the **Center for the Arts**, where there are art shows, dances, and other events. But SoMa's biggest attraction by far is the **San Francisco Museum of Modern Art** (151 3rd Street, tel: 415-357-4000; open Fri–Tues 11am–6pm, Thurs until 9pm, closed Wed), with its collection of 15,000 works, including those by Max Ernst, Picasso and Paul Klee. Designed by Swiss architect Mario Botta, many think the building overshadows the collections inside, but the museum is still worth a visit if only to admire the sunlight effects in the entrance hall beneath the five-story glass-roofed staircase. Be sure to leave time to visit the museum's gift shop.

Hanging out in Haight-Ashbury

Golden Gate Park: Away from the skyscrapers of Downtown, take the No. 5 Fulton bus to get to Golden Gate Park. Originally nothing but sand dunes, the area was turned into its present lush parkland quite by chance – or so the story goes – when 19th-century urban planner John McLaren accidentally dropped the oats from his horse's nosebag and they sprouted. McLaren carried on from there and today San Franciscans have a delightful landscape of small lakes and hills, an arboretum, botanical gardens, playing fields, stables, and a popular open-air chess hang-out. At the eastern end of the park there's a wonderful children's playground, and beyond it lies the **Haight-Ashbury** district of the 1960s 'flower children.' Although this is still a slightly depressed area, a regular infusion of stores and boutiques, along with steady 'gentrification,' promises continued improvement well into the future.

The park includes two major museums clustered around the Music Concourse. The M.H. de Young Museum is closed until 2005; its programs continue at the Legion of Honor in Lincoln Park. The very up-to-date **California Academy of Sciences** houses a natural history museum, an aquarium, and a planetarium. Afterward, you can rest in the lovely Japanese Tea Garden.

Alcatraz: Of the cruises available on San Francisco bay, the most interesting is to the disused prison of Alcatraz (tel: 415-773-1188 for information); be sure to bring a sweater as the air in the bay is nippy. Once on the island, park rangers conduct informative and witty tours of the former home of Al Capone and other convicts too hot for normal prisons. There are also excellent, award-winning audio guides, giving recorded reminiscences from guards and prisoners. Alcatraz – the name comes from the Spanish *Isla de los Alcotraces* (Isle of Pelicans) – is a 12-acre (5-hectare) rock with no arable soil. The water for the shrubs and trees growing today had to be brought in by the US Army, for whom it was a disciplinary barracks until 1934. A chilling 1½ miles (1.5km) of ice-cold treacherous currents, sharks, and raw sewage separate Alcatraz from the San Francisco shore. It was the ideal location for America's most notorious federal civil penitentiary, but enormously expensive in upkeep. In 1962, with each inmate costing $40,000 a year, Alcatraz was finally closed down.

Excursions from San Francisco

The Bay Area: Immediately north of San Francisco, at the southern tip of of Marin County, are the two charming little harbor towns of **Sausalito** and **Tiburon**, which you can reach either by car across the Golden Gate Bridge or by ferry. Tiburon is the quieter of the two, although both towns have a colorful Mediterranean atmosphere. Nearby you can see California's legendary Giant Redwood trees close up at the **Muir Woods National Monument**. Some of the trees are 1,000 years old and grow to heights of 250ft (75m).

Napa Valley

Wine Country: Wine lovers will enjoy a drive through the vineyards of **Napa Valley** and across the Mayacama Mountains to **Sonoma Valley**. Napa, less than 50 miles (81km) northeast of San Francisco, lies between the Mayacamas and the Howell Mountains, stretching from

Wine growing in this part of California is respectable enough for some of the best French Champagne makers to produce fine sparkling wines here.

the town of Napa in the south to Calistoga in the north. Highway 29 is the main route through the valley. The Silverado Trail, which runs parallel to it, is the slower, quieter, and more scenic route. Bus tours are available, and you can even fly over the vineyard in a hot-air balloon. The wineries provide tours and tastings in the cellars and organize picnics in the vineyards. Harvests begin around mid-August – California weather being so much more predictably sunny than in Europe.

Some of the larger wineries are at Sterling, and at Mondavi, Martini, Beaulieu, and Beringer in Napa, and at Souverain and Sebastiani in Sonoma Valley. Homesick French wine lovers may want to visit the Domaine Chandon in Napa, owned by Chandon of Moët et Chandon fame. The Hess Collection Winery near Napa exhibits artworks by Stella, Motherwell, and some of the ultra-realists painters. The smaller, family run 'boutique' wineries offer distinctive wines, with tastings in relaxed and informal showrooms. The Napa Valley Conference and Visitors Bureau, 1310 Town Center Napa, tel: (707) 226-7459 can help with maps and information. There's also a wine museum in town.

A word of warning: the best restaurants of the region tend to be closed on Tuesdays.

Pacific Coast: Take Highway 101 south from San Francisco and join Pacific Highway, Route 1, at Castroville, to get to **Monterey**, the old Spanish and Mexican capital of Alta (Upper) California. The bay was discovered in 1542 but was not settled until 1770, when Father Junípero Serra set up a mission here with the garrison protection of Gaspar de Portola's *presidio*. Monterey was a bleak, disease-ridden place, and Portola recommended it be handed over to the Russians, who also coveted it, 'as a punishment.' But Father Serra accepted the hardships and led the taming of the Monterey wilderness. His statue keeps watch on Corporal Ewin Road.

The town is proud of its past and offers a signposted tour of the Old Town's historic buildings from the 19th-century Mexican administration and early American period. The architecture is a mixture of Spanish adobe and American colonial clapboard, two storys with a balcony – an attractive-enough hybrid to earn it the name of 'Monterey style.' At the Chamber of Commerce, on Alvarado Street, you can get a map showing the major houses.

Look for the **Larkin House** at Jefferson and Calle Principal, home of the first (and only) US Consul, in the 1840s, and the **Robert Louis Stevenson House**, 530 Houston Street, where the writer lived while he was working on *Treasure Island*. On Church Street you'll find the site of Father Serra's original baked-mud church; rebuilt in 1795, it is now the **Royal Presidio Chapel** or Cathedral of San Carlos de Borromeo. To the left of the altar is an 18th-century *Virgin Mary* from Spanish Mexico.

Nearer the waterfront are the **Pacific House**, on Custom House Plaza, with a pleasant, flowery, and tree-shaded arcaded courtyard, and the **Custom House** (1827), taken over as the first US federal building on the Pacific coast.

More distinctively American is **California's First Theater** on Scott and Pacific streets, a pine-wood shack built by one Jack Swan in 1847 as a saloon with a dubious boarding house upstairs. Customers were (and still are) attracted by Victorian melo-dramas, but the 'boarding house' no longer operates.

Fisherman's Wharf, like San Francisco's attraction of the same name, is a collection of stores and restaurants out on the dock, but with a closer view of the boats. The fish here are almost always fresh, but not enough to keep Cannery Row as more than a weather-beaten curiosity.

Fisherman's Wharf, Monterey

The fisheries along the row were the sardine capital of the western hemisphere from 1921 to 1946, but by 1951 the sardines had disappeared. Today the timbered canneries made famous by novelist John Steinbeck as 'a poem, a stink, a grating noise' are restaurants, boutiques, and art galleries.

A big draw is the **Monterey Bay Aquarium**, featuring the denizens of the bay. With a wonderful Outer Bay exhibit holding a million gallons of water, this spectacular aquarium furnishes viewers inside and out with the likes of barracuda, leopard sharks, anchovies, and delicately lovely jellyfish. At feeding time divers don wetsuits and a microphone to talk to spectators while underwater.

Farther on, the scenic **17-Mile Drive** (27.5km) winds through the Monterey Peninsula (fee; motorcycles not allowed), but you can also drive south directly to **Carmel**, a delightful resort and former artists' colony ideal for a rest and serious shopping. Just out of town is the entrance to **Point Lobos State Park**, a com-

The spectacular cliffs of California's Highway 1

pact gem of statuesque wind-blown rocks and pocket beaches nestled among dramatic cliffs. Southeast of the town is the restored **Carmel Mission**, Basílica San Carlos Borromeo de Carmelo, where Father Serra is buried. The coast road from Carmel to Big Sur is only

There are several types of tours to San Simeon, including one that takes place at night. Lines can be long, but tickets are timed, so you can leave and come back again to enter immediately.

30 miles (48km) long, but it takes more than an hour of careful driving, and every hairpin turn reveals another spectacular vista.

Big Sur and the Pfeiffer–Big Sur State Park offer marvellous opportunities for picnics, camping, hiking, and fishing in the Big Sur River. The home of writer Henry Miller and other artists, Big Sur is a great place to escape the crowds.

The rugged shoreline road winds south for 65 miles (105km) more to where William Randolph Hearst, the man Orson Welles immortalized in *Citizen Kane*, built his dream home at San Simeon, now commonly referred to as **Hearst Castle** (guided tours; reservations advisable, tel: 800-444-4445). Hearst himself called the 123 acres (50 hectares) of castle, guesthouse *palazzi*, terraces, gardens, Roman baths, private zoo, and tennis courts 'the Ranch.' Building began in 1919 and had still not been completed when the tycoon died in 1951.

The 275,000-acre (110,000-hectare) estate lies 1,600ft (500m) up in the hills. After parking in the lot, you take a tour bus which drives past zebras, barbary sheep, and goats grazing on the slopes – remnants of Hearst's private zoo.

San Francisco architect Julia Morgan built 'the Ranch' to Hearst's specifications as a 'functional showcase' for his art collection. The range of the collection registers as you pass the 100-ft (30-m) swimming pool with its Greek colonnade and a copy of Donatello's Florentine statue of *David* on two 17th-century baroque Venetian fountains that Hearst had joined. Over the gigantic main entrance, in quiet simplicity, is a (genuine) 13th-century *Madonna and Child*.

Tinseltown

Los Angeles and Disneyland (*CALIFORNIA*)

Los Angeles is the quintessential modern creation. Only technology could have turned desert into one of the most flourishing metropolises on earth. Engineering genius brought water hundreds of miles across mountains and deserts to feed the city and its industry and nurture its lush gardens. The freeways arrived in time to link the people scattered across its vast area and create the burgeoning monster that never ceases to astonish.

People who don't know it complain that Los Angeles is nothing but a bunch of suburbs looking for a city. The cliché is not so much untrue as irrelevant to Angelenos. In the neighborhoods and townships that make up greater Los Angeles – Hollywood, Westwood, Santa Monica, Malibu, and dozens more – nobody's looking for a city; they know where they are. Up in the hills, down at the beach, in the valley, around the university campus, they're all integral parts of Los Angeles. Residents believe that LA is more a state of mind. A state of mind covering 460 sq. miles (1,191 sq. km), bounded by sand and sea to the west, mountains to the north and east, and desert to the southeast, all with an almost permanent canopy of sun. It's not surprising that leisure and pleasure are worshipped with little restraint here.

The Beach: The beach (Angelenos always refer to it in the singular) stretches some 40 miles (65km) from Malibu south through Santa Monica, Venice, Marina del Rey, Hermosa, and Redondo to Palos Verdes before the sands hit the pollution of Los Angeles Harbor and the Long Beach shipyards. There's no better way to get the special feel of Los Angeles than to go straight there. In LA, beaches are not just resorts for holidays and weekend cottages, they are year-round residential areas.

Malibu is home to the more relaxed members of the film community. The town sits in the 30-by-5-mile (48-by-8-km) Santa Monica Mountains National Recreation Area, a wonderland of federal, state, and county parks with nature trails overlooking fabulous beaches. Stop at the Visitor Center in Thousand Oaks for orientation. Malibu Lagoon's Surfrider Beach attracts surfers worldwide, while Las Tunas and Topanga beaches are a little more peaceful. Malibu Pier is a good place to fish.

Built on more solid ground, **Santa Monica**'s beaches are more of a family affair. But it is neighboring **Venice** that attracts all the attention. The beach and beach park here are a non-stop open-air amateur circus of freaks, acrobats, weight-lifters, clowns, and jugglers. In 1892, millionaire Albert Kinney wanted to create on the Pacific coast a replica of Italy's Venice, complete with canals, gondolas, a *palazzo* or two, hotels, and amusement arcades. Then somebody discovered oil and the idea was abandoned. Four canals remain with a Lighthouse Bridge that traverses the lagoon area feeding the canals. The neighborhood has revived as a diverse community of serious artists, upscale galleries, laid-back movie folk, and the ever-present bohemian types.

Bladers on Venice Beach

Grauman's Chinese Theatre

Hollywood: London buries its heroes in Westminster Abbey, Paris puts its great to rest in the Pantheon, and Los Angeles offers the hand, foot, and hoof prints of its stars in the cement courtyard of the fabulous **Grauman's Chinese Theatre** (6925 Hollywood Boulevard). So it's not a bad plan to start a Hollywood pilgrimage here. Sid Grauman had the idea in 1927 of getting the immortals' prints when they attended premieres at his exotic cinema. Most followed the example of the Marx Brothers and Rita Hayworth: they got on their knees and made a handprint. But it was natural for Fred Astaire to leave a footprint, and cowboy Tom Mix preferred leaving the hoof print of his horse.

Adjoining Grauman's is the **Kodak Theatre**, home of the Oscars and part of the **Hollywood-Highland** complex. Tours can be taken where backstage guides provide the low-down on the gossip and the glitz. They take place daily from 10.30am–2.30pm and last half an hour, tel: 323-308-6363.

Then walk along **Hollywood Boulevard** (this is one part of LA where walking is customary) and you'll see over 2,500 actors' names on bronze stars embedded in the pavement – the famous **Walk of Fame**. In the beautiful old art deco Max Factor building nearby is the **Hollywood History Museum.**On several levels in this museum are costumes and location sets that most movie fans will recognize instantly, including the outrageous sets from *Moulin Rouge*, and in the basement, the spine-tingling cell of Hannibal Lecter from *The Silence of the Lambs*.

You'll pass Frederick's of Hollywood with its lingerie museum, and the beautifully restored **Roosevelt Hotel**, the site of the first public Oscars ceremony. Between La Brea and Western Avenue, the boulevard has the tacky splendor of the 1920s and '30s, with its low, flat stucco buildings and droopy palm trees. The **Hollywood Entertainment Museum** (7021Hollywood Boulevard, tel: 323-465-7900; open daily) has sets from *Star Trek*; interactive attractions and a dizzying 6-minute retrospective film of clips from scores of movies.

A few blocks north of the boulevard is **Hollywood Bowl** (2301 North Hollywood Avenue, tel 323-850-2000), the wonderful open-air auditorium where the Los Angeles Philharmonic Orchestra holds concerts against a background of the gigantic illuminated letters of the **H-O-L-L-Y-W-O-O-D sign** planted up in the hills. Across the street from the entrance is a big barn that serves as the **Hollywood Heritage Museum**.

Running south of Hollywood Boulevard is Los Angeles' most famous street, **Sunset Boulevard**. The Hollywood section of Sunset is known simply as 'the Strip.' It's where people cruise in convertibles, and where sleazy nightclubs and cheap motels vie with upscale boutiques and elegant restaurants.

Downtown LA: the heart of LA culture and political life is to be found around the **Civic Center** and **Broadway**, an area bordered by First and Temple streets, and North Main Street and North Grand Avenue. When it was first built in 1928, **City Hall** (200

Hollywood's Kodak Theatre

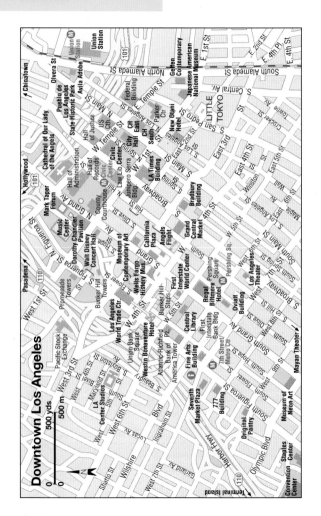

Downtown Los Angeles

North Spring Street) was the tallest building in the city until height restrictions were lifted in 1957. An observation deck is open weekdays from 10am till 4pm. A few blocks northwest of Civic Center is the **Music Center**, LA's cultural complex. As well as housing two theaters and being home to the LA Philharmonic, the Music Center is the site of the **Walt Disney Concert Hall**, designed in futuristic style by noted architect Frank Gehry. Northeast of Civic Center, near Olvera Street and art deco **Union Station**, are some of the city's oldest buildings. The **Avila Adobe** has been restored and can be visited.

The historic theater district on Broadway has evolved into a bustling Hispanic shopping street, well supplied with electronic goods and bridal gowns. A remnant of the proud theatrical past is the **Million Dollar Theater** (307 South Broadway), decorated with whimsical terra-cotta. The **Mayan Theater** (11th and Hill Street) is now a nightspot. From a terminal located on Fourth and Hill streets, the **Angels Flight** inclined railway carried downtowners up and down Bunker Hill. Opened in 1901 as the 'Los Angeles Incline Railway,' the funicular has been restored but had to close following an accident in 2001.

Not far away, the **Museum of Contemporary Art** (MOCA) contains art created since the 1930s. The colorful Mexican life of the city can be sampled at **Grand Central Market**, north of Pershing Square. (The other great food market is **Farmer's Market**, west of Beverly Hills at Fairfax and Third.) West of Downtown is another great thoroughfare, **Wilshire Boulevard**, which has become a living museum of the city's art deco architecture from the 1920s and 30s.

Beverly Hills: exclusive and assertively separate from Los Angeles, Beverly Hills' streets are lined with Rolls Royces and Mercedes, the architecture of the mansions an astonishing mixture of Spanish, Gothic, Bauhaus, and Renaissance.

The town is phenomenally clean; littering is almost a capital crime. It's policed with formidable efficiency and, except for in the great shopping streets such as **Rodeo Drive**, walking is

Close encounter at Disneyland

viewed with suspicion, especially at night. If you do want to take a walk here, it's a good idea to put on tennis or jogging clothes; the police will assume you're doing athletics. Only burglars, it seems, walk around Beverly Hills in 'normal' clothes.

Universal Studios: (Lankershim Boulevard, north of the Hollywood Freeway; open daily 9am–7pm) offers an elaborate tour in open trolleys with guides who have all the showbiz flair of Hollywood itself. Participating in the special effects trickery, you'll be attacked by spaceships and the shark from *Jaws*, you'll meet a three-story King Kong, and experience all the earthquakes, flash floods, and fires you ever saw in disaster movies. You'll visit sound stages and back lots and learn the screen techniques used to create film's great illusions. You'll see how Moses parted the waters of the Red Sea in *The Ten Commandments* and ride through a 'town' that includes a New England fishing village, a Bavarian square, French bistros, and an Italian pizzeria, all in the space of four blocks.

Disneyland: (Anaheim, 27 miles/44km southeast of downtown LA on the Santa Ana Freeway, tel: 714-781-4565, <www.disneyland.disney.go.com>). Since 1955, Walt Disney and his successors have been dispensing the good clean pleasures of a make-believe world inspired by the fantasies of his movies. Applying the techniques of the cinema and advanced electronics technology, Disney takes you around this smiling technicolored theme park on outings that are simply stupefying in scope and impact. You can buy a one-, two-, or three-day Passport that covers the whole Disneyland complex, which is good for unlimited use of the attractions.

Pick up a booklet with maps at City Hall and head down **Main Street**, which sets the tone with its sunny evocation of small-town USA. You may notice that all the houses and stores are three-quarter size. In this effort to escape from the realities of the outside world, everything is a little smaller than life-size, and larger than life. Don't linger in the stores: head for **Fantasyland**, with Sleeping Beauty Castle, Pinocchio's Ride, and a boat cruise through the charming, disarming 'It's a Small World.'

Adventureland is a boat ride through simulated jungle foliage on a river that passes successively through Asia, Africa, and the South Pacific, complete with plastic tigers and alligators. A miniature railroad takes you through **Frontierland**, the pioneer country of the Old West where a loudspeaker warns you to 'watch out for Indians and wild animals.' Just the faintest unease is aroused by a settler's cabin on fire with a wax-model pioneer lying outside, killed by an s arrow. But at the end of each ride are reassuring ice-cream and soft-drink stands.

One of the most exciting themes is **Tomorrowland**, which is constantly being renovated to keep pace with progress. The rides include a submarine, the head-spinning Space Mountain, Star Tours, and some of the most up-to-date experiments in public transportation.

A recent Disney attraction is a theme park in its own right. **Disney's California Adventure** traces the history and social culture of the Golden State with a series of thrill rides, cowboys, and themed 'lands,' including one on Hollywood.

Museums in Los Angeles

Museum lovers have much to be excited about in southern California. The **LA County Museum of Art** (5905 Wilshire Boulevard, tel: 323-857-0098), designed by William Pereira, is one of the largest of its kind in the country. The permanent collections include Impressionist paintings, contemporary art, Indian and Islamic art, American art, and the Armand Hammer collection of Roman glass. In addition, the Pavilion for Japanese Art and the sculpture garden also contain some outstanding works, and there are regularly changing exhibitions of contemporary art.

The **Norton Simon Museum** at Pasadena (411 West Colorado Boulevard, off the Ventura Freeway, tel: 626-449-6840) contains a collection of European paintings, drawings, and sculpture from the early Renaissance to the 20th century, along with Indian bronzes and Asian stone carvings.

The UCLA **Armand Hammer Museum of Art** (10899 Wilshire Boulevard tel: 310-443-7000), the legacy of yet another billionaire, contains the world's largest collection of Daumier's works, in addition to much other Western European art.

The **Getty Center** (1200 Getty Center Drive, tel: 310-440-7300) is LA's arts and cultural complex, perched on a 110-acre (44-hectare) site in the Santa Monica Mountains. Designed by architect Richard Meier, the sprawling campus includes the Getty Research Institute's 750,000-volume research library and houses the Getty Museum's permanent collection of paintings, illuminated manuscripts, and French decorative arts. The setting, the campus and the view are worth the visit, although the collection is surprisingly modest. Admission is free, but advance parking reservations are required.

The Getty Center

San Diego (*CALIFORNIA*)

It was at San Diego that Portuguese captain Juan Rodríguez Cabrillo first set foot on California soil in 1542. Sixty years later, its bay was explored by the Spanish, but it wasn't until

1769 that Father Junípero Serra built his first mission.

The best way to appreciate San Diego's beauty is from the sea. Take a **cruise** along the bay – they start from Harbor Drive at the end of Broadway – past the man-made Harbor and Shelter islands around the tip of the peninsula to Point Loma out on the Pacific. Back on dry land, you can visit one of the 19th-century ships moored on the Embarcadero as part of the Maritime Museum Fleet, the most picturesque being the iron-hulled square rigger, *Star of India*, built in 1863. Or drop into Seaport Village, a lively complex of stores, restaurants, and galleries.

Hotel del Coronado

San Diego's discovery is celebrated by the **Cabrillo National Monument** on the Point Loma promontory (follow the signs southwest on Rosecrans Street). Cabrillo's statue, donated by the Portuguese government, faces the spot at which he landed.

Old Town (bounded by Juan, Twiggs, Congress, and Wallace streets) is a six-block area of restored adobe buildings from the city's Mexican era, plus the brick houses of early American settlers. You'll enjoy a rest under the palms and eucalyptus trees of Plaza Vieja, originally the center and bullring of the old pueblo. The **Gaslamp Quarter**, a mostly Victorian neighborhood downtown is another popular spot for strolling. Victorian architecture reaches its zenith on the nearby Coronado peninsula, where the extravagant **Hotel del Coronado** (1888) has a distinguished guest list that has included everyone from John F. Kennedy to Britain's Prince of Wales.

Heading upcountry

The modern town is blessed with enlightened urban planning, the popular **Horton Plaza** shopping center, and the wonderful **Balboa Park**. Set right in the center of town, the park offers a wealth of sports facilities and many of the city's cultural attractions. There's even an Elizabethan playhouse, site of the summer Shakespeare festival.

But the star of the park is the **San Diego Zoo** (2920 Zoo Drive, hours vary seasonally), justly acclaimed as one of the world's finest. Certainly it's one of the most humane, giving the animals as large and natural a living space as possible in the confines of a man-made park. Australian species are particularly well represented. You can skim over the zoo in the Skyfari aerial tramway or take a guided bus tour.

Another great park is at **Mission Bay**, with first-class aquatic amenities. Paddle around tiny islands and lagoons in canoes, or sail in catamarans and full-size sloops. It is also the home of **Sea World**, where you can see the famous 3-ton killer whale, not to mention sea lions, otters, and a walrus.

California National Parks and Monuments

The best times of the year for Yosemite and Sequoia are spring and autumn. Winter offers good cross-country skiing in Yosemite and lovely snowscapes in Sequoia, but check ahead to find out which roads are closed. Summer in both parks is crowded, but the peace of the high country is always within reach. Death Valley is best from late autumn to early spring. In the height of summer, temperatures can rise to 100°F (37°C) or even higher.

Yosemite: 'Base camp' – which might be a plush hotel room, modest lodge accommodations, or simply a tent – is at the heart of **Yosemite Valley** along the Merced River. From the valley you can hike, bicycle (rentals at Yosemite Lodge or Curry Village), ride a horse or mule, or take the shuttle bus to all the sights. Soaring granite cliffs enclose the valleys: **Half Dome** at the northeast end (8,842ft/2,695m); Glacier Point, Sentinel, and Cathedral Spires down the south wall; and **El Capitan**, Three Brothers, and Washington Column up the north wall.

You can grade the hikes according to your capacity and endurance. In the Merced River Canyon, **Vernal Falls** is within the scope of any normally healthy person. A well-marked path begins at Happy Isles Nature Center, where knowledgeable US Rangers will answer your questions. If you're up to it, push on along the Mist Trail, past Emerald Pool to **Nevada Falls**, and you'll begin to lose the crowd. Here you're on the John Muir Trail, named after the Scottish naturalist who explored the Sierra Nevada mountains and made their conservation against the encroachments of civilization his life's work. The trail passes Merced Lake to the lovely **Tuolumne Meadows** in the high country. The final destination is Mt Whitney over 200 miles (320km) away.

Less exhausting is a drive or shuttle-bus ride past Badger Pass to **Glacier Point**, 7,214ft (2,199m) above sea level. Both the altitude and the view over the whole valley and the High Sierras beyond are breathtaking. You can see Yosemite Creek drop

Bridal Veil Falls, Yosemite

half a mile (1km) from the opposite wall in two spectacular plunges (Upper and Lower **Yosemite Falls**) and also get an outstanding view of majestic Half Dome. From here you can hike and picnic on your way back along the Panorama Trail via the Nevada and Vernal falls – 8 miles (13km) downhill in all.

Another beautiful hike is out to **Mirror Lake**, especially in spring or early summer when the waters are perfectly still in the early morning or at sunset, capturing the marvelous colors from the trees and Mt Watkins behind.

Sequoia/Kings Canyon: A haven of peace and contemplation among the giant sequoias, the largest living creations on earth, many of them nearly 3,000 years old. The forest offers a gorgeous array of dogwoods, sugar pines, and white firs, and a rich flora of orange leopard lily, white corn lily, lupine, chinquapin, and bracken fern. This is no place for a hurried look; walk slowly, sit quietly, and listen; fall asleep under a tree. Watch for the birds – woodpecker, raven, spotted owl, but also W.C. Field's favorite, the mountain chickadee, and the Steller's jay.

Start at the **Giant Forest Village** with its motel and the Park Rangers' Visitor Center at Lodgepole where you can get a map and information about the best walks in the forest and hikes in the back country. The best introduction to the forest is the **Congress Trail**. It's an easy 2-mile (3-km) walk that begins at the **General Sherman Tree**, the biggest of them all, 275ft (84m) high, 103ft (31m) around its base and still growing. Reaching up for the light well above the rest of the forest, the branches start 130ft (40m) above the ground. As you move among the other great sequoias – the President, the Senate Group, the House Group, and the General Lee – you can understand John Muir waxing lyrical about 'the first tree in the forest to feel the touch of rosy beams of morning and the last to bid the sun goodnight.' Another beautiful walk, by no means an exhausting hike, is out to **Crescent Meadow**, passing more of the stately giants along the way.

If you want to get away and explore the back country, carry on along the High Sierra Trail running 11 miles (18km) from

Crescent Meadow to **Bearpaw Meadow**. This is not too formidable a hike. A nearby lake and streams offer good trout fishing, and there's a fair chance of spotting some of the park's bobcats, coyotes, golden eagles, black bear, spotted skunk, and cougar.

Death Valley: A convenient way to see Death Valley is to combine it with a trip to Las Vegas. Come from the east, either on Highway 95 and via Death Valley Junction on Route 190, or farther north via Beatty, on Route 58.

This desert is perhaps the greatest surprise of all the wonders of California. It's not one but a dozen landscapes, not a monotonous expanse of sand dunes but an endless variety of terrains, rock formations, colors, and plants. Come here in winter and you may see a flood of spring flowers blooming in the wake of the sparse rains. But above all, there's the light, uncannily clear, distorting distances, pink at dawn, white at mid-morning, piercing silver at noon, and then shimmering into gold as the afternoon progresses.

Death Valley

Don't be deterred by the name Death Valley. It was bequeathed by unlucky Gold-Rush hopefuls who crossed from Arizona and Nevada and suffered bitter hardships here. There are now some excellent facilities at **Furnace Creek**. However, if you are crossing the desert in summer, do not drive off the main road and, if you break down, wait in your car for the next police patrol. Also take plenty of gasoline and drinking water.

Get up at dawn – really, you won't regret it – and drive out southeast along Highway 190 to **Zabriskie Point**. As the sun rises and the light hits Tucki Mountain and the tips of the Panamints to the west before plunging into the valley's primeval salt-lake bed below, you're likely to be set wondering about the world's creation. By mid-morning (if you visit in winter) the temperature could be something like a cool 50°F (10°C) on your exposed ridge, but walk down the hill to the lake bed and you'll feel the heat rising to meet you, reaching the 80sF (20sC) by the time you get to the bottom.

Continue over to **Dante's View** (altitude 5,745ft/1,751m), looking down at **Badwater**, 282ft (86m) below sea level, and the lowest point in the United States. Make up your own mind whether this is paradise, purgatory, or hell. On the other side of the valley are Wildrose, Bennett, and Telescope peaks.

Craps, a popular Las Vegas game

Las Vegas (NEVADA)

If European and American dreamers go to California, where do Californian dreamers go? Well, they take Interstate 15 from Los Angeles northeast across the Mojave Desert and over the Nevada state line to Las Vegas. While once the resort may have been considered Sodom and Gomorrah with neon lights,

The Great Pyramid and the Sphynx at 'Luxor'

today it seeks to project a wholesome image as host to international conventions and major sporting events, welcoming millions of tourists in the process. The metro area has a resident population of over 1 million people – mostly in fancy retirement complexes – that enjoys a wealth of cultural and sports amenities offered by the area's health clubs, art centers, and churches. But despite its supposed squeaky-clean aura, Vegas remains one of those myth-laden towns that everybody should visit at least once.

At **Casino Center** in the downtown area, which has banks and professional buildings cheek to jowl with casinos, the neon lights are so bright that midnight can look like noon back in the Mojave. Focus for all the action is **Fremont Street**, or 'Glitter Gulch.' Every lit-up window shows dozens of people tugging the levers of the 'one-armed bandit' slot machines. One neon sign declares: 'For every US coin you got, we got the slot.'

Downtown is also the site of the spectacular **Fremont Street Experience** (hourly after dark). The eye-popping overhead display is five city blocks long, and uses 2 million light bulbs and 200 loudspeakers for a 10-minute multimedia show of graphics,

Las Vegas has it all – showgirls at Bally's

music, and video. A cartoon of evolution from the jungle is followed by jet fighters, dancing girls, and musical instruments. This free show is definitely the best value in Vegas.

The famous Las Vegas **Strip** (officially Las Vegas Boulevard), between Sahara and Tropicana avenues, is a solid 4 miles (6.5km) of hotels and casinos, each with a nightclub advertising America's top stage productions, comedians and singers, and a score of girlie shows – on ice, in water, even on an ordinary stage. Although in 2003, Las Vegas stopped aggressively marketing itself as a family destination, there's still plenty of wholesome entertainment around, too, including several theme parks. Some of the major hotels also provide family entertainment, and food and accommodations are priced low (subsidized by gambling profits).

An evening walk along The Strip offers more entertainment than most cities can provide in a week. These are the true monuments of Las Vegas; the re-creations in casino form of the Great Pyramid and the Sphynx at **Luxor**; the Piazza San Marco and Grand Canal in the **Venetian**; and the scaled-down pastiche of the Manhattan skyline in **New York-New York**. There are palaces of the Orient, ancient Rome, Persia, Paris, and other places of exotic fable. **Bellagio** is an Italianate marvel, styled after the shoreline at Lake Como with its immense and elegant fountain display; **Caesars Palace** offers the decadent style of ancient Rome with fountains and Italian marble colonnades. And there's much, much more to see: the **Tropicana**'s island paradise; the belle-epoque style **Monte Carlo**; the medieval **Excalibur**; the **Mirage**'s gardens, waterfalls, palm trees, and the regularly erupting, street-side volcano. **T.I.** (Treasure Island) has an hourly sea battle featuring cannon fire, healthy, scantily-clad females and swashbuckling male pirates.

All this decor is there to provide an exhilarating backdrop to the gambling – hundreds of slot machines spill out from the casinos into the lobbies, plus roulette tables, baccarat, blackjack, and bingo. Poker is usually played in a roped-off area at amazingly sedate tables attended by house dealers too busy keeping the game going to crack a joke. The most enjoyable tables for spectators are the dice or craps games. Players get very excited as the 'bones' roll. They whoop, cheer and groan as their fortunes change. Two things that you won't see in the casinos are clocks or windows – the management doesn't want you distracted. As a result, the action is non-stop. Come to be amazed.

Seattle (WASHINGTON)

Bright and energetic, Seattle, in Washington state, is blessed with one of those natural locations that render public relations superfluous. Its bay on Puget Sound is surrounded by the green, green country of Washington. The snow-capped Olympic and Cascade mountains loom in the background and 14,410-ft (4,392-m) Mt Rainier towers over them all. The climate is fresh and moist, hence the town's sobriquet of the 'Emerald City.' In spring and summer the place positively sparkles.

Seattle's fortunes were very much tied to those of the Boeing aircraft manufacturers, as the lumber industry, which got the town started in the 1850s, began to decline. But Bill Gates's Microsoft, amazon.com and a whole host of other dot commers took the city to unprecedented prosperity. The deepwater Pacific harbor has made a natural gateway for trade with Asia, and the city benefits from a lively Chinatown as well as a Japanese community. It was also the springboard for the Alaska and Klondike gold rushes of the 1880s and 1890s.

Pioneer Square (First Avenue and Yeslerway) is the only vestige of the good old days. Its Victorian red brick has been spared the urban developers' wrecking ball, and the pleasant tree-shaded little square is surrounded by some good restaurants (both expensive and moderate), quality boutiques, and excellent jazz clubs.

You can explore Seattle's lower depths on an **Underground Tour** (from 608 First Avenue, tel: 206-682-4646 for reservations). It leads through the subterranean city that was burned out in 1889 and buried under today's sidewalks, streets, and buildings, which were simply erected on top. You'll see old stores and facades and eerie galleries, illuminated by the guide's amusing stories of the town's beginnings.

Take a ferry from the waterfront

Like any self-respecting port, Seattle is liveliest along the **waterfront**. Seafood restaurants, fish stands, and chandlers share the area along Elliott Bay with parks and the **Seattle Aquarium** (Pier 59, tel: 206-386-4300; hours vary seasonally). Stop by to feast your eyes on octopus, sharks, eels, seals, and salmon, or watch a film on the watery depths in the Omnidome theater. Afterwards, when it's time to get out on the water yourself, harbor tours (Pier 56) and a variety of ferry rides (Pier 52) will fit the bill.

Also on the waterfront, **Pike Place Market** (Pike Street and First Avenue) presents stands where farmers, fishmongers, and butchers sell their own produce. It's delightful to see views of the water through huge piles of

It's easy to travel around the Pacific Northwest. From Seattle, you can take a train to Portland, Oregon, or on to San Francisco. Heading north, jump aboard an excursion boat to Victoria, in Canada.

tomatoes or flowers. The **International District**, bounded by Fourth and Eighth avenues and Main and Lane streets, includes Chinatown and the Japanese neighborhood. You'll find lots of jade and jewelry stores here, as well as great restaurants, a Buddhist temple, and the **Wing Luke Asian Museum** (407 Seventh Avenue South, tel: 206-623-5124; open Tues–Sun), which traces the history of Asian and Pacific Island immigration to the US over a 200 year period, and hosts many temporary exhibitions.

The great symbol of Seattle is the 607-ft (185-m) **Space Needle** (tel: 206-905-2100; open Sun–Thurs 9am–11pm, Fri–Sat 9am–midnight), standing on a tripod. This is a proud relic from the 1962 World's Fair. The revolving restaurant and observatory at the top give splendid **views** across the city to the Olympic Mountains and the Cascade Range dominated by Mt Rainier. Right below the Needle is the **Seattle Center**, which also grew out of the World's Fair. It's buildings consist of an Opera House, a playhouse, the Coliseum, two theaters, a sculpture garden, three first-rate museums and much more. The center merits a visit on its own.

The **Pacific Science Center** (tel: 206-443-2870; open daily) is a spectacular structure housing exhibits on space exploration, laser technology, the rich Northwest Indian culture, but above all the oceanography of Puget Sound. The **Seattle Asian Art Museum** (a branch of the Seattle Art Museum in Volunteer

Park) features contemporary American and regional artists, and major traveling exhibitions. A recent addition is the fabulous **Experience Music Project** (tel: 206-770-2700; open daily until 8pm in summer; until 6pm on winter weekdays; until 8pm winter weekends. Closed Mon in winter). Sponsored by Microsoft's Paul Allen, the EMP is a unique state-of-the-art interactive museum celebrating the creative process in pop music. The remarkable building, designed by Frank Gehry, is said to resemble the inside of a guitar. Fans of Jimi Hendrix (Hendrix was born near Seattle) should plan to spend at least a day here, and even casual fans will probably while away several hours.

If the silhouette of Mt Rainier (14,410ft/4,392m), an active volcano encased in over 35 sq. miles (90 sq. km) of snow and ice, has proved too inviting to resist, why not take an excursion out to the **Mt Rainier National Park**? It's only two hours south of town, and there are exhilarating hikes to be enjoyed.

Far West States

Alaska: This is the largest state in the USA, encompassing a vast area of infinite variety. A popular misconception is that it is all a frozen wasteland. The **southeastern Panhandle**, from Ketchikan via Juneau up to Haines and Skagway, has a moderate climate, a lot of rain, and fertile land, with considerable forests. The **Gulf Coast**, north and west of Haines around the Gulf of Alaska, is the most densely populated, centering on Anchorage, the state's only real metropolis.

The **Western region**, including the Alaskan Peninsula and the Aleutian and Pribilof islands, is foggy, wet, and windy; great for sea- and bird-life. The **Interior** south of the Brooks Range from the Canadian Yukon border toward the Bering Sea has a dry climate and is hot in summer, bitterly cold in winter. And the Arctic, extending from Kotzebue above the Seward Peninsula in the west around Barrow to the North Slope at Prudhoe Bay, has a bleak landscape of permanently frozen soil.

A great way to see Alaska is by boat. Ships cruise from Seattle and (in summer) Vancouver, San Francisco, and Los Angeles.

Somewhere over the rainbow in Hawaii

Hawaii: The 50th and newest state of the US is an archipelago of seven inhabited islands and a collection of islets, reefs, sand-bars, and rocks strung out over 1,500 sq. miles (2,430 sq. km) in the North Pacific. The state's capital, Honolulu, is a modern high-rise city on the island of **Oahu**. The long white beaches and blue ocean are perfect for swimming and sunbathing. Surfers swear by the waves on Oahu's north shore. Waikiki offers the most vigorous nightlife.

The island of **Hawaii** is known locally as the 'Big Island' because of its size and to distinguish it from the state name. The main feature is the volcanoes, particularly the still-active Kilauea Crater. **Maui** has wonderful beaches and plenty of sports facili-ties, as well as the old royal capital of Lahaina. A visit to the 10,000-ft (3,000-m) dormant volcano Haleakala is a must.

Farther north, the islands of **Molokai** and **Lanai** are ideal for those who want a quiet vacation – ideal opportunities for hiking, mule-trekking, or rugged jeep trips. **Kauai**, the Garden Island, is a lush tropical paradise, whose rivers and waterfalls are a delight for fishing enthusiasts.

WHAT TO DO

The diversity of America offers almost every kind of recreational activity; cultural, sporting, or artistic, and at a level as rarified or as popular as your taste or budget requires.

Outdoor landscapes of all kinds provide immense scope for climbing, swimming, hiking and bicycling. Spectator sports are played at world class. Although team games are mostly American varieties – baseball, basketball, ice-hockey, and American football – they all offer displays of terrific skill and entertainment. Theaters and showrooms can engage with everything from *Chicago* to the Ring Cycle to Bruce Springsteen. Most of the world's cuisines are well represented, and American regional kitchens concoct delights and delicacies from the abundance of American farms and fishing grounds. What to do in America? Whatever you like; how long have you got?

SPORTS

Few countries are more sports conscious than America. The competitive spirit runs high in every activity, and facilities are first-rate. The Atlantic coasts of New England, New York, New Jersey, the Carolinas, and Florida, and the Pacific coast of California provide every imaginable kind of **watersport** – swimming, diving, boating – and they're inventing new ones every season. For surfing, snorkeling, scuba diving, windsurfing, and waterskiing there are stores at the seaside resorts where you can rent the necessary equipment. Inland towns like Chicago or Detroit provide similar facilities on their lakes and rivers.

Long-time reputations hold that southern California or Hawaii are best for **surfing** and the Florida Keys best for **scuba diving**. For surfing, the best waves are to be found at Malibu on Point Duma and Surfrider at Santa Monica State Beach north of the pier, and at La Jolla on Windansea and Boomer.

Left, catching the wild surf in Hawaii

For **sailing**, Long Island Sound (New York and Connecticut), Cape Cod (Massachusetts), Newport (Rhode Island), the Chesapeake Bay (Maryland and Virginia), and Fort Lauderdale (Florida) are among the best on the East Coast, while Pacific sailors swear by San Diego (California) and Seattle (Washington).

Canoeing, a leisurely sport in the Florida Everglades, becomes an exhilarating test of endurance on the Colorado River in Arizona and Utah or in Yellowstone Park.

Deep-sea **fishing** provides high adventure in the Caribbean waters off Florida, but it's equally satisfying up around Cape Cod, along the Outer Banks of North Carolina, or off the northern California coast.

For freshwater fishing, check with local information centers for licensing regulations. **Hunting** in the Rockies for moose, elk, and gamebirds is carefully regulated but by no means forbidden. Check with the local tourist information or park rangers for information about hunting permits.

Hiking has become a major sport in these health-conscious times and there are marvelous opportunities in the national parks of the West or in the hills of New England. The famous Appalachian Trail runs all the way from Maine down to Georgia. It's the best way to get away from the crowd.

Summer in Yosemite

Wear good walking boots, not just tennis shoes, for the longer hikes, and warm clothing is good for the sudden cool evenings in the mountains. The rangers who run the national parks can help you with maps for the more interesting nature trails.

If you want to try **mountain climbing,** it's always best to go with an experienced guide, especially over unfamiliar terrain. You can usually rent equipment in the national parks. Call the park rangers for information.

Jogging is still a popular pastime, and healthiest of all when done barefoot along a sandy beach. The town parks often have marked trails with exercise stations en route. In Boston, for instance, the parks, which locals call their 'emerald necklace' strung along both banks of the Charles River, are perfect for jogging. If you want to get around a little faster, you can rent a **bicycle** or maybe even a pair of **rollerblades**.

Tennis, **golf**, and **squash** are also popular. Tennis has grown to such an obsession that many towns provide

Good powder can be found most of the year round

floodlit public courts for nighttime matches. Frequently the larger hotels will have at least one tennis court on their grounds, and sometimes they can help you with access to the local golf clubs. It's a good idea to take your home golf-club membership card, but there are also many municipal golf courses open to the public.

Horseback riding is good in New England and California. In the national parks, it's one of the more satisfying ways to get off the tourists' beaten path.

If you're taking a winter vacation, **skiing**, both cross-country and downhill, is spectacular in Colorado, Utah, and California, but there are also first-class family resorts in New England. You may find the après-ski a little slow, but the slopes are fine and the people more disciplined at the ski lifts than in Europe.

Spectator Sports

Don't let the unfamiliarity of **American football** or **baseball** discourage you from watching these exciting games. An hour of the raucous humor of a baseball crowd for the New York Yankees or the Boston Red Sox, the militant religious fervor of football fans at a Dallas Cowboys game, or the stoical fatalism of Chicago Bears' supporters will teach you more about the local community than any sociological monograph.

Other sports, such as **basketball** and **ice hockey**, are played out in a particularly electric atmosphere, charged up by a lot of gambling on the 'points spread' (points difference between the two teams) in the one and by the violent body contact in the other. This is the stuff of Roman circuses. In comparison, the American version of soccer is rather tame.

Just what modern America can do to the once sedate game of **tennis** is best witnessed at the US Open Championships at New York's Flushing Meadow in September. The only thing

Football players in action

drowning out the roar of the jumbo jets flying over from La Guardia Airport is the clamor of the spectators. And yet the tension somehow brings the best out of the players.

An unusual sport played in Newport, Rhode Island, and in Florida is **jai alai** (pronounced 'high lie'), a local version of the high-speed Basque game *pelota*. It's played in a three-walled court, trapping and hurling the ball with a scooped reed-basket known as a *cesta*. Night

Baseball – the field of dreams

games are played at the Biscayne Fronton in Miami.

Horse racing attracts some colorful characters to Aqueduct and Belmont in New York and to Santa Anita in Los Angeles. But the great moment of the racing year is in Louisville for the Kentucky Derby (pronounced Der-bee) in May. If you are in the country at the time but can't get to Louisville, you can still attend one of the countless Kentucky Derby parties held around the country, often in neighborhood bars. Several hours are spent drinking mint juleps (bourbon with crushed ice, sugar, and fresh mint), while the race itself lasts just two minutes.

SHOPPING

The most important advice we can give you on shopping in the US is not to start on your first day or you may find you'll have to go home early. For Americans, the business of seducing the consumer has become a fine art, and shopping is more or less the national pastime. America is also the home of the 'outlet store,' and these bargain bazaars can offer some of the best cures in retail therapy.

Exclusive shopping in Rodeo Drive, Los Angeles

Outlet stores have become so established now that outside most major towns and cities are outlet malls – clusters of discount sheds. The outlets provide end-of-line and last season's fashion goods and famous-label designer gear. Polo Ralph Lauren, Nike, Swatch, Gap, Liz Claiborne, Banana Republic all make regular appearances in outlets and outlet malls and offer great savings for style-slaves.

East Coast Shopping

Europeans find **New York** discount prices, widely advertised in the Sunday papers, advantageous for cameras and electronics. In the realm of gadgets, Hammacher Schlemmer (147 East 57th Street) and The Sharper Image (4 West 57th) reign supreme with such extravagant oddities as electronic weighing machines that talk to you in the bathroom. The ultimate toys store is F.A.O. Schwarz (Fifth Avenue and 58th Street; GM building).

Manhattan's department stores are an exciting world of their own. Bloomingdale's now has two branches; Barneys continues to innovate styles and trends, and then there's ever-popular Macy's, which bills itself as the world's largest store.

Boston's importance in the nation's history makes it an ideal place to find the best of old Americana, but it becomes increasingly difficult to get the authentic stuff without historic prices. In antiques shops in Charles Street on Beacon Hill or Harvard Square in Cambridge you'll find original, sturdy early furniture, but more often good reproductions. Patchwork quilts are another specialty of colonial days, as well as decorative lacy-patterned glassware and handmade pewter. Although whaling days are over, you can still find delicately carved scrimshaw made from whalebone and walrus tusks (particularly in curio shops in Back Bay or around Cape Cod and on Nantucket). Fragrant green candles made from bayberries are a specialty of Cape Cod.

Washington is a terrific museum town, and the museums also provide the best place to buy unusual and attractive gifts. The Air and Space Museum store has great model aircraft and spaceships for children and the young at heart. The Museum of Natural History has jewelry of semiprecious stones and beautifully mounted pieces of rare minerals. The main Smithsonian Bookstore, in the Museum of American History, offers a comprehensive selection of the country's arts, history, and technology. Near the Mall entrance, take time to browse through the museum store, which sells replicas of the more popular exhibits of old Americana.

Macy's always pulls in the crowds

The National Geographic Society (17th and M streets NW) is also well worth visiting for its wonderful maps and picture-books of places near and far. For posters of the great masters, art calendars, and art books, try the stores at the National Gallery of Art, both East and West, and the Hirshhorn.

Study the newspapers, especially the Sunday editions, which are usually filled with advertising about the sales or 'specials' currently promoted in the big stores. The major cities have discount stores, particularly good for records, cameras, electronic equipment, and sporting goods. The press also gives details of local flea markets, generally held only on weekends.

West Coast Shopping

San Francisco is a fine place for shopping. Several small shopping centers, such as The Cannery, Pier 39, or Ghirardelli Square are clustered around Fisherman's Wharf. These may specialize in tacky tourist junk, but among all the tee-shirts are some out-of-the-ordinary souvenirs: colorful dragons to hang in the wind, unusual toys, bizarre sunglasses or 'food art,' perfect for the next party. One place worth traveling for is Ghirardelli's Chocolate Shop. Goodies are made on the premises and exported all over the United States, and you can buy dark or white chocolate in almost every imaginable form. More mainstream shopping is centered around Market Street and Union Square. Macy's and other department stores are here, together with

---

Garage Sales

A fine American institution for bargains in second-hand goods is the garage sale. Families moving away or just periodically emptying out their attics and cellars offer old clothes, furniture, books, records, and ornaments, displayed in the driveway of their garage. Track them down from hand-written advertisements posted on walls, lampposts, or supermarket notice boards, or by just driving slowly around residential neighborhoods on summer Saturdays – you're bound to find half a dozen. They're great places to discover a particular type of old Americana – ashtrays, car license plates, tobacco tins – that Americans consider junk and Europeans consider collectibles.

smaller retailers, jeans stores and antiques shops. For top fashions and amusing bric-a-brac, try elegant Union Street.

Los Angeles glitters with conspicuous consumption, and few places shine as brightly as Rodeo Drive. Two complexes here draw in the beautiful and the wealthy: the Rodeo Collection, a pinkish mall on two levels specializing mostly in fashion, and the faux-cobbled winding street Two Rodeo Drive, home to Tiffany, Cartier, and Dior.

A mile (1.6km) to the east is Century City, where the shopping center and marketplace has stores, theaters, and restaurants whose validation will give you three hours of free parking. The Beverly Center at La Cienega Boulevard and Third Street has neon escalators that ascend five floors of stores and theaters. The highly attractive Santa Monica Mall has a pedestrian-only street lined with stores and sidewalk cafés. The enclosed area features a score of different food counters and dining at central tables.

As with most things, **Las Vegas** is investing vast sums of money in order to make Sin City the most exciting retail experience in the world. Its enclosed malls are truly fabulous – resplendent with Moorish domes, flying birds, ceilings that 'rain,' sunsets that change color, talking statues, and just about every gimmick imaginable. When it all becomes too much, fit young people on rickshaws are on hand to pedal weary shoppers from retail center to restaurant. The Fashion Show Mall contains enough indoor retail space to display real automobiles, announcing its presence on the Strip with a gigantic outdoor 'cloud.'

ENTERTAINMENT

In New York, Boston, Philadelphia, Washington, Chicago, San Francisco, and Los Angeles, the **opera**, **ballet**, and **symphony concerts** are major events of the social calendar. You have to plan well ahead to get tickets for these, but it's worth the effort. Your travel agency will probably be happy to help you contact the relevant city visitors information centers and arrange advance bookings.

The best **theater** is still in New York, but other major cities have good repertory groups and experimental drama, particularly where there's a large university.

Dance clubs continue in force, though with more varied music (even golden oldies) than the monotonous but hypnotic 1970s stuff. **Nightclubs** range from the spectacular extravaganzas of Las Vegas with top-flight singers and comedians, to the seedy strip joints (both male and female) of San Francisco, to quiet supper clubs with a dance band, or just a piano bar in the smarter hotels. Jazz is king in New Orleans. New comedians try out on Sunset Strip in Los Angeles or in Greenwich Village, New York. And satirical cabaret knocks everything it can lay its hands on in Chicago. In Miami's Little Havana they dance in the streets. In Texas, some of the nightclubs offer electronic bucking broncos and mud wrestling. But fashions change as fast as the light bulbs.

If you're a **movie** buff and like to be ahead of your crowd some American movies that open in Europe in the autumn or at Christmas are released in the US during the summer. This used to be regular practice, but now with the growth of DVD's lead times are shortening. Another great cultural phenomenon is the all-night **television**, a good way of curing your jet lag.

Nighttime in New York

If you could do justice to nighttime New York, you'd never have the energy to see it by day. But that's why they call it 'the city that never sleeps.' Pick up a copy of the *Village Voice,* the *New Yorker* or *Time Out New York* to find out what's happening.

Theater is still Broadway, on side streets between West 44th and 50th streets for the big show and big ticket prices. Off-Broadway and Off-Off-Broadway shows are smaller and less expensive. New York is one of the world's dance capitals. The excellent resident companies – the New York City Ballet, Robert Joffrey, Merce Cunningham, Alvin Ailey, Paul Taylor, Dance Theater of Harlem, and the American Ballet Theater – also attract the competition of the very best foreign companies.

Opera is almost as richly endowed, with the huge classical

Blues legend Buddy Guy playing at his club in Chicago

resources of the Met and the more modern repertoire of the New York City Opera, both at Lincoln Center. The New York Philharmonic is the flagship for the 30 or so classical music concerts held on any one evening – with the added summer delight of free Philharmonic and Metropolitan Opera performances in the city's parks. Cinema is also well provided for in Manhattan. The Film Society of Lincoln Center features programs of film retrospectives and hosts the autumn New York Film Festival. On the nightclub scene, which only really livens up after midnight, there is a wealth of music, especially in the clubs in Greenwich Village, the Meatpacking District, and on the Lower East Side. For a quieter night, go dancing under the stars at the supper clubs in the hotels around Rockefeller Center.

Unless you need to see the season's smash hit, you can usually pick up theater tickets at the box office a few days in advance (weekdays only). Head for TKTS (47th Street and Broadway) for half-price seats on the day of performance. Alternatively, buy a copy of the *New York Times* or one of the magazine mentioned above, and order tickets online or by mail.

Nighttime in Washington

The Kennedy Center for the Performing Arts is Washington's cultural star. In a beautiful location on the banks of the Potomac River, it is also the country's most prolific entertainment venue, with more than 3,000 performances held in its five theaters. The National Symphony is a first-class orchestra. The National Theatre, which opened in 1835, stages Broadway hits and one-man performances by the famous.

For tickets pick up an out-of-town copy of the *Washington Post* before you get to town – best of all, the Friday edition with the 'Weekend' section – to plan and book ahead for plays, operas, and concerts. Otherwise you can try for returned tickets at the box office an hour before curtain time.

Nighttime in San Francisco

For nightlife, San Francisco is much more fun than Los Angeles; Los Angelenos tend to entertain at home in private. But San Franciscans go out a lot, and the coffee houses and streets are bouncing with vitality most nights.

Bars in San Francisco are a whole way of life – downtown Irish bars on Geary, Italian coffeehouses in North Beach, and a host of late-night waterfront 'joints' along Embarcadero to Fisherman's Wharf. There is no obvious distinction to be made between 'tourist traps' and local hangouts, perhaps because San Franciscans are enthusiastic tourists in their own town, so you'll be mixing with the locals wherever you go. Some bar-cafés around North Beach specialize in good amateur opera singing – you'll hear it as you walk by. If it sounds like Pavarotti or Callas, it probably is – played on the jukebox between 'sets.' The San Francisco Opera is very good, but you'll need to book ahead for a seat.

Broadway is also the main thoroughfare for jazz **nightclubs** and 'topless,' 'bottomless,' and other forms of strip joint. The South of Market District, or SoMa, is home to a dynamic club scene; you'll be able to dance the night away in places that stay open until the sun comes up.

Calendar of Events

January 1 New Year's Day.

January 15 Martin Luther King's Birthday.

Last Sunday in **January** is Super Bowl Sunday. The climax fo the American football season is the biggest sporting event in the US.

February, Chinese New Year the starting date varies. Celebrations go on for a week. The largest parades are in San Francisco.

February 2 Groundhog Day; the groundhog awakens from the winter, and goes outside to see if he sees his shadow. If he does, there will be six more weeks of winter and he goes back to sleep. Otherwise spring is just around the corner.

February 14 Valentines Day.

February 17 Presidents' Day.

March Mardi Gras (Fat Tuesday), also known as Shrove Tuesday, falls between February 3 and March 9. Celebrations are legendary in New Orleans, but also take place all along the southern gulf coast, and with no less enthusiasm and revelry.

March 17 St Patrick's Day. Celebrated all over America, the largest events are in New York and Savannah.

Last Monday of **May** is Memorial Day, to commemorate fallen service men and women.

June 14 Flag Day.

July 4 Independence Day. Celebrated with barbecues, picnics, and family gatherings, and spectacular fireworks displays in cities across the US.

The first Monday in **September** is Labor Day.

September 17 Constitution Day.

Second Monday in October Columbus Day, also known as Discoverer's Day.

October 24 United Nations Day.

October 31 Halloween. The biggest celebrations are in San Francisco and New York.

November 11 Veteran's Day.

Fourth Thursday in November is Thanksgiving Day, to commemorate the Pilgrims' survival of their first hard year in the New World.

December 31 New Year's Eve.

EATING OUT

America is a country of cuisines as diversified as its ethnic groups. Texas draws on its Mexican beginnings for spicy chili and barbecued dishes, and Florida takes inspiration both from Cuban rice dishes and Jewish delicatessen. Still, all the way from Maine in the Northeast or to the state of Washington in the Northwest, you'll find the same straightforward vegetable soups, plain green salads, steak and potatoes, fruit pies, and ice cream. The great mobility of Americans has spread the original unadorned, often rather bland European cooking right across the country. This basic unity of taste has guaranteed the phenomenal success of the fast-food franchises. But most areas have distinctive cuisines, notably New York, California, Miami, New Orleans, and the Pacific Northwest.

One note for Europeans; genetically modified food is very common in the US and not labeled. Foods that are not labeled as 'organic,' especially fast foods, are often GM.

What to Eat

Sandwiches: Usually served on white, rye, pumpernickel, or wholewheat bread, a roll or a bagel (doughnut-shaped rolls), or perhaps on *pita*, Arab flat bread. Classic fillings include chicken, tuna, and egg salads; lox (smoked salmon) and cream cheese, a delicious Jewish specialty served on a bagel; corned beef or pastrami (a kind of cured beef), also Jewish specialties. Club sandwiches consist of three slices of toast in layers filled with turkey, lettuce, tomato, bacon, and sometimes cheese. Hoagies, heroes, submarines, po' boys, and grinders all refer to the same thing: a fat, mouth-stretching sandwich of French bread, stuffed with meatballs, sausages, or ham-cheese-salami-onions-lettuce-peppers-tomatoes, and olive oil.

Soups: Vichyssoise is a chilled soup of leeks, potatoes, and onions; chili con carne, often served as a soup, is in fact a spicy stew of kidney beans, ground beef, onions, and tomatoes.

Salads: The simplest salad consists of iceberg lettuce and a few slices of tomato and cucumber, but many American-style restaurants nowadays feature a self-service salad bar with an attractive assortment of greens, garnishes and breads. Your choice of dressings may include 'tomatoey' French, Thousand Islands (mayonnaise, ketchup, hard-boiled egg), Russian (mayonnaise and chili sauce), Italian (oil, vinegar, garlic, and herbs), or Roquefort. The 'chef's salad,' which may contain ham, cheese, and chicken, is a meal in itself; raw spinach salad with mushrooms ranks as a great American original; Caesar salad has romaine lettuce, Roquefort cheese, and a raw egg in the dressing; coleslaw (cabbage salad) often appears with sandwiches. Cold pasta salads often served with crisp raw vegetables or seafood are also very popular.

Meat: Beef still takes first place – though in health-conscious America the trend is away from red meat. It comes in enormous portions and is almost invariably tender. In steakhouses, you often pay a flat rate for a steak, a baked potato with sour cream or French fries (chips), a self-service salad bar, and in some cases a glass or two of wine, or beer.

'Spare ribs' are pork ribs, marinated in a spicy sauce, baked or broiled, and eaten with your fingers.

Fish and seafood: Fish and shellfish are often of excellent quality, both the ocean fish of the East and West coasts and the Gulf of Mexico and the freshwater fish of the mountain rivers and lakes. In fish, look out especially for red snapper, bluefish, marlin, and swordfish. Great seafoods include soft-shell and steamer crabs, especially from Maryland, Dungeness crab and Maine lobster.

Vegetables: In these health-conscious days, organic vegetables are plentiful, and excellent farmed produce is widely available. More specialty stores and restaurants open almost every day, offering vegetarian, vegan, and gluten- or dairy-free options.

Cheese: Swiss-, Dutch-, and British-style cheeses are manufactured in Wisconsin, New York, and Vermont; the sharper ones approach their European equivalents. The French cheeses, imported or locally imitated, tend to be too pasteurized to approximate their taste on the other side of the Atlantic, but the creamier versions are spiced with herbs and garlic. Cheese boards are often served in French restaurants, and cheese-and-wine bars are spreading.

Desserts: Ice cream is undeniably where America excels. Amazing flavors are invented every minute, and the range just intoxicates the palate – spearmint, peanut butter, apple pie, cinnamon – and the vanilla is often terrific too. Put it on the fruit pies, *à la mode*, and you're heading for a blissful calorific

Lunch alfresco in California

catastrophe. Apple Brown Betty is a kind of apple crumble. Brownies are a good, rich chocolate cake usually served in small squares. In early summer when the strawberries are at their peak, strawberry shortcake – scone-like biscuit on the bottom with dollops of whipped cream on top – can be sublime. Enjoy things, you're on holiday.

Regional Cuisine

Some of the best **New York** restaurants are in the theater district, the East Side, Upper West Side, or in trendy SoHo and TriBeCa. But rather than be told where to go *this* year, just consider the variety.

The town benefits enormously from its cosmopolitan tradition. Italian restaurants are legion. With the French, you have to choose carefully between the few authentic – and very expensive – establishments and run-of-the-mill operations. The Chinese are much more reliably competent and more varied in their regional cuisines, especially down in Chinatown itself. There are Greek, Spanish, Japanese, Jewish, Mexican, Brazilian, and Indian restaurants. Increasingly, they're taking their exotica out on to the streets, vending Arab *falafel* sandwiches, spicy Indian *samosas,* or Turkish *shish-kebab* in hot competition with the local pretzels and hot dogs.

New York's own contribution to the world of gastronomy begins with the hot dog, which you can have either with sauerkraut or fried onions but not, authentically, without mustard. The deli sandwich is a special Broadway institution, naming permutations of turkey, corned beef, pastrami, bacon, lettuce, tomato, or whatever else. The New York strip steak is a good, thick cut of tenderloin, best eaten rare. Long Island Blue Point oysters are too good to spoil with the cocktail sauce that inevitably accompanies them. Manhattan clam chowder has tomato in it (as opposed to the creamy New England type). Although cheesecake may have come from Central Europe, it never tasted better than since it reached Brooklyn and the delis on Broadway.

New Englanders are proud of their culinary specialties. In **Boston**, start your day with some of the 'home-baked' muffins offered at breakfast time. Blueberry, cranberry, apple, and date nut are among the more interesting varieties. Or breakfast on pancakes swimming in maple syrup. By all means be sure to try Boston baked beans. Simmered in molasses with a chunk of salt pork, this hearty dish is said to have been a decisive factor in the British abandoning their American colonies.

If that's true, then the French must have been delighted at becoming America's first allies for the chance to sample the lobster freshly caught off the coasts of Maine and Massachusetts.

Thanksgiving

The fourth Thursday in November is one of the most significant holidays on the US calendar. It is celebrated to signify a successful harvest after the first hard winter by the Pilgrim fathers, who invited the Native Americans to share in their bounty. Although there is some doubt as to the historical accuracy, Thanksgiving has an affirming resonance of the original pioneering spirit. The celebration is also a time for families to gather from all over the country or the globe, and is often more important than being together at Christmas.

Festive food traditionally centers around roast turkey with chestnut stuffing, gravy, and cranberry sauce. Winter vegetables – sprouts, parsnips, and potatoes – are usually served as an accompaniment. There is no traditional drink, but dessert is almost always pumpkin pie, with a few regional variations.

They are simply delicious boiled or steamed with melted butter, or grilled on a barbeque. The oysters, too, are excellent, as are the haddock, sea bass, flounder, and scrod (local white fish, usually young cod).

For dessert, as in the rest of America, fruit pies are legion, but the cranberry is a New England innovation. Boston cream pie is actually a sponge cake filled with custard and glazed with chocolate icing. For real local authenticity, try the Indian pudding, made from cornmeal, molasses, and milk.

New Orleans justifiably prides itself on some of the most distinctive cooking traditions in America. It certainly is evocative of the city's own personality– or could it be that the city derives its personality from the cuisine: rich, Latin, and spicy? There are two quite distinct culinary styles particular to New Orleans, and around Louisiana: Creole and Cajun.

The name 'Cajun' refers to descendants of French-Canadians, and is a contraction of 'Acadian.'

The Creole tradition combines a French love of intricate sauces, the Spanish penchant for mixing fish, meat, and vegetables with rice, and a taste developed in the West Indies and in Africa for liberal seasoning with hot peppers. It's usually served up with a dash of good old-fashioned Southern cooking and hospitality, just for good measure.

Gumbo, a West African word for okra (the green vegetable sometimes known elsewhere as 'lady's fingers'), is the basic ingredient and generic name for thick soups of chicken or seafood, a meal in itself. Crayfish, pronounced and often spelled in Louisiana 'crawfish,' best served straight boiled, is a favorite springtime shellfish to which whole festivals are devoted in April.

Oysters here are plentiful and relatively inexpensive, encouraging New Orleans chefs to prepare them in numerous and marvelous ways: fried or in gumbo; as oysters Rockefeller – rich as its name implies, baked with spinach and breadcrumbs;

or oysters Bienville, cooked in white wine with shrimp, mushrooms, and shallots – or oysters *en brochette*, oysters skewered and wrapped in bacon; they're also a special delicacy raw.

Cajun cooking is from the more country-style cuisine favored among the fishers and farmers of the bayou. Fish soups like the spicy courtboullion, spicy sausages like boudin and andouille, and the world famous classic, *jambalaya*.

Jambalaya is a *paella*-like dish of rice and chicken, crab, or shrimp with bits of sausage or ham, pepper, and tomato. The poor man's version is the simple red beans 'n' rice; red

American service – style with a smile

kidney beans and rice flavored with pork, deliciously filling.

The local variation on the all-American submarine sandwich is the 'po-boy' (long) and muffuletta (round), French bread stuffed with cold meats, oysters, or other seafood, cheese, and salads, often pepped up with spice to local taste.

Figure-conscious **California** is, of course, the place where healthy eating first became popular. Using the huge variety of locally produced ingredients, the state came up with something called 'California cuisine,' which emphasizes both freshness and simplicity and at the same time represents a fusion of California's melting-pot culture. In this, it is the very essence of modern American cooking.

The **Pacific Northwest** has an abundance of superb fresh ingredients, from vegetables and fruits to meat, fish, and seafood,

New York's Tavern on the Green

and they have enough varieties of cuisines to serve them all at their best advantage. There is also the wonderful diversity of ethnic influences to draw culinary inspiration from Europe, Canada, and the whole of the Pacific Rim. The result is a lip-smacking smorgesbord of culinary melodies with themes from Japan and South-East Asia as well as French Canada and the United States.

What they all have in common is the light touch that allows the excellent ingredients to shine through. That and the salmon. Copper River, sockeye, wood-smoked – there are more kinds of salmon here than you can shake a rod at.

Ethnic Food

Nearly every large city has its Little Italy, Chinatown, neighborhood Jewish-style delicatessen, and Mexican restaurants. On the West Coast you'll find a wonderful Italian version of bouillabaisse, a thick fish soup known as *cioppino*, more fish than soup, with every available shellfish spiced up or down, according to taste. Pizza is ubiquitous throughout the US, but its style changes from region to region.

Chinese restaurants offer many variations of Chinese regional cooking – Peking, Szechuan, Shanghai, Hunan, as well as the familiar Cantonese. It's worth calling up a day in advance to order a whole Peking duck, glazed with honey and roasted slowly with spring onions. This gentle delicacy finds a sharp contrast in the spicy smoked duck you might try in a Szechuan or Hunan restaurant. But don't overlook seafood. The steamed sea bass, prepared with green onions, black beans, garlic, ginger, and sesame oil, or the Szechuan shrimp are served hot in both senses of the word.

Thai and **Vietnamese** restaurants have sprung up from coast to coast, offering subtler, spicier variations on the well-known Oriental staples of rice and noodles. In Thai houses look out for the spicy fish dishes, delicious green curries and soups ranging from delicately aromatic to devastatingly hot.

Japanese restaurants, particularly *sushi* (deliciously fresh raw fish, served in bit-sized cuts with rice) have made a place for themselves all over the US. Perfectly cut yellowfin, salmon, smoked eel, and tuna, accompanied with warm *sake* (Japanese rice wine) is winning friends all over the states. Also look out for Japanese noodle bars and *teriaki* (a marinade used for fish, seafood, meat or poultry).

Mexican eating houses offer an array of crispy *tacos* and *tostadas* and moist *tortillas* (cornmeal pancakes) stuffed with shredded beef or chicken, grated cheese, avocado, and lettuce. But the best dishes are more substantial and sophisticated, such as *mole poblano* (chicken with almonds, sesame seeds, peanuts, chilies, raisins, and savory chocolate sauce).

Jewish food features Eastern European borscht, cabbage soups (red or green) with sour cream, gefilte fish, and minced fish balls. Blintzes, a crisper version of the Russian blini, are folded over minced meat as an appetizer or sweet cream cheese as a dessert. Corned beef and spicy, smoked, Rumanian-style pastrami makes delicious sandwiches; it's served on rye bread with potato salad and pickled cucumbers.

The all-you-can-eat salad bar is a mainstay of US restaurants

What to Drink

Seattle – the birthplace of Starbucks – was the town that redefined the morning coffee ritual the whole world over. Typically, Portland claims to have pioneered the path in the gourmet coffee business, but that could just be an example of an old Portland-Seattle rivalry. Either way, both towns can boast innumerable small independent 'boutique' coffee shops, as there are all over the Pacific Northwest. You can try dozens of varieties of beans, blends, and roasts, espressos, mochas, and lattes without ever having to step into a chain outlet or franchise.

Cold drinks are invariably served iced. If you want a good serving of cola or lemonade in the coffee shops and fast-food places, specify 'little ice.' Beer is, of course, also served ice cold, but without the ice.

Wines from California have gained acceptance worldwide. The days are past when a Napa Sonoma or Anderson Valley winery was considered an also-ran by the sommelier. Fine wines from Northern California are now well established on wine lists and menus. Oregon is also making news in the wine business here, particularly with some high-end reds. Be prepared for some surprisingly high prices in restaurants, though. Sometimes a good French, Italian, or Spanish wine can be less expensive on the wine list than a comparable or indifferent American offering. You can order domestic wines by the bottle or, in many places, by carafes or single glasses as the 'house wine.'

Since Americans have discovered wine, hard liquor has diminished in fashion – but not the cocktail hour. Cocktail bars abound, and more bars offer cocktail menus. Dry martinis (gin or vodka and a few drops of dry vermouth) can be potent. Bourbon, a mellow whiskey from Kentucky or Tennessee, is made of corn (maize), malt, and rye; drink it straight, on the rocks, or with soda. Many bars promote late-afternoon 'happy hours' when two drinks are served for the price of one. Another attraction for spirit drinkers is that American bartenders often serve very friendly measures.

New Orleans claims to have invented the cocktail, or at least the word. It is, they say, a distortion of the French for egg-cup, *coquetier*, in which a Creole bartender by the name of Antoine Peychaud served his brandy and bitters in the 19th century. The dictionary, a little more soberly, suggests that cocktail was originally 'a horse of racing qualities, but not a thoroughbred.' That could also serve as a fair description of two local specialties: the Sazarac is rye whiskey or bourbon and bitters served in a glass coated with anisette; the Ramos Gin Fizz adds sugar, lemon, lime, orange-flower water, egg white, crushed ice, and soda water to the gin. If you're still conscious, try a *café brûlot*, coffee flavored with cinnamon, cloves, orange peel, and *flambé*.

American beers have also risen above the gassy, industrial, canned brews of old. Brewpubs and microbreweries have sprung up all over the country. Treats are in store for fans of the fermented hop from Washington state to California, and all the way across America to New York state.

Pretty as a peach in Georgia

HANDY TRAVEL TIPS

An A–Z Summary of Practical Information

A

ACCOMMODATIONS

Hotels and motels: It's always wise to make accommodations reservations in advance, and you can do this directly through the nationwide toll-free reservation services operated by the large hotel and motel chains (listed in the *Yellow Pages* of the telephone directory).

American hotels and motels usually charge by the room, not by number of occupants. Rates indicated normally do not include the state and city sales taxes or daily occupancy tax. Most rooms have air-conditioning, a private bathroom, and television.

You normally have the choice of twin or double beds and motel rooms often have two double beds – convenient for family travel. Most resort hotels offer special rates to guests who take their meals on the premises: A.P. (American Plan) includes three meals a day and M.A.P. (Modified American Plan), breakfast and lunch or dinner.

Motels are one of America's great bargains. Many belong to national chains, so you can book a whole trip in one go.

Country inns: These are often large, luxurious, older but beautifully restored properties. Guests tend to stay for more than just one night and dinner is a fairly formal affair, usually eaten with the other residents in the dining room. Country inns can be expensive.

Guest houses and **bed-and-breakfast inns:** These tend to be fancier and pricier than their European counterparts and are found in smaller towns and holiday centers. Local tourist authorities have extensive lists.

Ranches: Ranches in America can mean far more than just cowboys, campfires, and horses. There are luxury ranches, enormous complexes with all facilities including swimming pools and tennis courts, and the simpler – but nevertheless comfortable – dude ranches, where guests take part in everyday ranch and cowboy life. For further information, contact a travel agency. Budget accommodations can be found on farms and family ranches; local tourist authorities have lists.

Hostels: These are the most inexpensive accommodations, sometimes located outside towns, and are open to members of national youth hostel organizations. For further details, contact your national youth hostel association or go to the website of Hostelling International-USA at <www.hiusa.org> for information on membership and a list of hostels near the US town or state you want to visit.

YMCA and YWCA: a number of centrally located residences are run by the YMCA and the YWCA. Rates are quite reasonable. Membership is not necessary, but demand is high so make reservations two months ahead; tel: (800) USA-YMCA or (312) 977-0031; or <www.ymca .net> (go to 'Find Your YMCA').

Students and young people can find inexpensive accommodations at university campuses and through local student associations.

Camping: Camping in America generally involves some kind of recreational vehicle – campers, motorhomes, or trailers (caravans), although in some areas you are allowed to just arrive and pitch a tent. Campgrounds are divided into two categories: public (found in the national parks, state parks, and state forests) and private. Almost all facilities have running water; some even have restaurants. Sites in the most popular parks must be booked directly with the individual lodge, anywhere from eight weeks to a year in advance, depending on the season. If you are sleeping rough, you must obtain a permit from the park.

AIRPORT INFORMATION (See also GETTING THERE)

Boston: *Logan International (BOS)*, 3 miles (5km) east of business district. Airport bus service to major hotels every 30 minutes during the day; travel time 20–30 minutes. Shuttle bus (Massport) to subway (Blue Line) service every 15 minutes during the day; travel time 15 minutes. Shared-ride van service to Boston and surrounding towns. Free airport bus to Water Shuttle runs every 15 minutes during daylight across inner harbor to downtown Boston. Subway and Water Shuttle are recommended over car or bus due to frequent traffic jams at Sumner Tunnel.

Chicago: *O'Hare International* (ORD), 18 miles (29km) northwest of the Loop. Bus service to downtown hotels every 10 minutes during the day. CTA Blue Line subway every 15–30 minutes during the day, every 60 minutes at night. Transfer to *Midway Airport* using Omega Airport Shuttle.

Los Angeles: *Los Angeles International (LAX)*, 16 miles (26km) south of central business district. Airport bus service to downtown Los Angeles, Hollywood, Beverly Hills, Westwood, etc., every 10–20 minutes during the day. Numerous connections to surrounding areas. Private door-to-door shuttles are also available, tel: (800) 650-8441, (800) 400-8060, or (310) 782-6600. Transfer to *Van Nuys Airport* every 30 minutes.

Miami: *Miami International (MIA)*, 7 miles (11.5km) west of downtown Miami. 'Super Shuttle' minibus service available; travel time 15 minutes, tel: (800) 874-8885. Municipal buses run regularly from the airport bus station (on the first level of concourse E, opposite US Customs) to Miami and Miami Beach; however, there is no luggage space provided. Transfer by coach to *Fort Lauderdale Airport* takes 60 minutes.

New York area: *John F. Kennedy International (JFK)*, 15 miles (24km) southeast of midtown Manhattan. Hotel limousine and minibus service at intervals throughout the day. Express bus to Grand Central Terminal, Penn Station, and the Port Authority Bus Terminal every 30 minutes; a separate free shuttle service operates from the Grand Central stop to major midtown hotels. The journey time from JFK takes from 60 to 70 minutes. Helicopter to citywide heliports every 30–40 minutes during the day. Transfers by bus from JFK to *La Guardia* are every 30 minutes, by limousine to *Newark International* (45–75 minutes). There's an inter-airport helicopter service (10–15 minutes depending on airport). Yellow Taxi Service is fixed at a flat rate, plus tolls and tips. Air Train is an airport rail system that connects JFK and Newark airports with the region's public transportation. Go to <www.airtrainjfk.com>. *Newark International (EWR)*, 16 miles (26km) to midtown Manhattan, taking 40–60 minutes depending on traffic and time of day. New Jersey Transit buses depart to New York Port Authority Bus Terminal every 15 minutes between 6am and 1am. Other buses depart every 20–30 minutes and stop at both Grand Central

Terminal and Penn Station. Transfers to JFK and La Guardia airports are available by bus at Port Authority or by train at Penn Station <www.panynj.gov>. For information on the AirTrain, go to <www.airtrainnewark.com>.

San Francisco: *San Francisco International (SFO),* 14 miles (22km) south of downtown near the town of San Mateo. There is no subway to the city, but shuttle buses are frequent; call the Airport Transportation Line, tel: 1-800-736 2008 for details.

C

CLIMATE AND CLOTHING

The US climate varies from frozen north to southern sunbelt, so take your destination into account as you pack. In summer, it's warm pretty much everywhere – except northern New England, Oregon, and Washington. One city anomaly is San Francisco, where spring and summer can be surprisingly chilly. In winter, heavy outer wear is essential, except in the southernmost states. For New York and Chicago, rubber overshoes are a good idea, or long underwear. Even in Florida and California, temperatures can plunge to freezing in December, January, and February, but cold spells never last long and can be followed by a heat wave. North and south, air-conditioning takes the edge off summer heat and humidity, so have a jacket or light wrap handy for the chilly indoors.

Monthly average maximum and minimum daytime temperatures in degrees Fahrenheit:

		J	F	M	A	M	J	J	A	S	O	N	D
Chicago	max.	32	35	45	59	70	81	84	83	76	65	48	35
	min.	17	20	29	40	50	60	65	64	56	46	33	22
LA	max.	67	68	69	71	73	77	83	84	83	78	73	68
	min.	47	49	50	53	56	60	64	64	63	59	52	48
Miami	max.	76	77	80	83	85	88	89	90	88	85	80	77
	min.	59	59	63	67	71	74	76	76	75	71	65	60
New York	max.	39	40	48	61	71	81	85	83	77	67	54	41
	min.	26	27	34	44	53	63	68	66	60	51	41	30

And in degrees Celsius:

		J	F	M	A	M	J	J	A	S	O	N	D
Chicago	max.	0	2	7	15	21	27	29	28	24	18	9	2
	min.	-8	-7	-2	5	10	16	18	18	13	8	1	-6
LA	max.	19	20	21	22	23	25	28	29	28	26	23	20
	min.	8	10	10	12	13	16	18	18	17	15	11	9
Miami	max.	24	25	27	28	29	31	32	32	31	29	27	25
	min.	15	15	17	19	22	23	24	24	23	22	18	16
New York	max.	4	5	9	16	22	27	29	28	25	19	12	5
	min.	-3	-3	1	7	12	17	20	19	16	11	5	-1

COMMUNICATIONS

Post offices: The US postal service deals only with mail; unlike in other countries, you cannot cash checks or make international telephone calls. Post office hours are from 8 or 9am to 5 or 6pm Monday to Friday, and from 8 or 9am to noon or 1pm on Saturday. Some branches have longer hours. Smaller branches close one afternoon a week, often Wednesday; all are closed on Sunday. Stamps can also be purchased from vending machines in drugstores, and in air, rail, and bus terminals, but you will pay a surcharge.

General delivery: (also known as 'poste restante'). Mail marked 'General Delivery' can be sent to you care of the main post office of any town. Letters will be held for no more than a month. American Express offices also keep mail for 30 days; envelopes should be marked 'Client's Mail.' Be sure to take a drivers license or passport for identification.

Internet and faxes: Most hotels are equipped to deal with the internet or faxes – at a price. Most office-services stores have internet access or can send faxes for a lower price, or try a document copy store such as Kinko's. Or even public libraries. Wireless internet access is becoming more commonplace every year; New York's Union Square and all of the Lower Manhattan area is now wireless.

Telephones: Public telephones can be found just about everywhere. Directions for use are on the instrument. Call rates are listed and explained in the front of the general directory or White Pages. Evening (after 5pm), night (after 11pm), and weekend rates are generally lower. For Information (directory inquiries) call 411. All long-distance calls require you to punch '1' before the three-digit area code for direct service. Be aware that in some heavily populated areas, like Greater Las Vegas, it's necessary to dial the entire area code even if it's a local call with the same code. For operator assistance punch '0.' All numbers with an 800, 888, or 877 prefix are toll-free (no charge). Always dial 1 before the 800. For information on toll-free numbers dial 1-800-555-1212.

Long-distance and many international calls may be dialed direct, but are very expensive at pay phones. You can save money with a phone card from a drugstore. Look for cards for around 10¢ per minute or less.

CONSULATES

Every major US city has consulates to serve foreign nationals. Here are the ones in New York. Consult the phone book for those in other cities.

Australia:	150 East 42nd Street, New York 10017; tel: (212) 351-6500
Canada:	1251 Avenue of the Americas (at 50th Street) New York, NY 10019; tel: (212) 596-1628
Ireland:	345 Park Avenue (at 51st Street), New York, NY 10022; tel: (212) 319-2555
New Zealand:	780 Third Avenue, New York, NY 10017; tel: (212) 832-4038
South Africa:	333 East 38th Street, New York 10016; tel: (212) 213-4880
UK:	(British Consulate General) 845 Third Avenue, New York, NY 10022; tel: (212) 986-2200

CRIME AND THEFT

Crime rates are falling in many major American cities. Petty theft and non-violent crime are still commonplace though, and crimes of violence still occur. Follow a few common-sense rules, relax and enjoy yourself.

• Keep valuables and reserves of cash, travelers' checks, etc., in a hotel safe. Carry only what you need from day to day. Be sure your purse (handbag) is securely fastened and keep your wallet in an inside rather than hip pocket. Never leave belongings unattended – at an airport, in a store, on the beach, or on view in a car.

• If you are in unfamiliar territory, inquire if any neighborhoods are unsafe. After dark, stay where the crowds are.

• If you are driving, keep car doors locked and windows up, lest some malefactor leap in when you're stopped at a traffic light. By the same token, never drive around with the windows wide open and your purse or valuables on the seat: an invitation to some snatch-and-grab artists.

• As in most countries, be on the alert for pickpockets and bag-snatchers in any crowded area.

CUSTOMS AND ENTRY REGULATIONS

Many foreign visitors need a visitor's visa, which can be obtained at any US embassy or consulate. British visitors and other Europeans with a valid ten-year passport and a return ticket do not need a visa for stays of less than 90 days. But as security measures become stricter, be prepared to be finger-printed and your eyeballs scanned on arrival. Everyone must fill out customs declaration forms (usually distributed by your airline near the end of the flight).

The following chart shows certain duty-free items you, as a non-resident, may take into the US (if you are over 21 where alcohol is concerned) and, when returning home, into your own country:

Into:	Cigarettes		Cigars		Tobacco	Spirits		Wine
USA	200	and	100	or	2 kg.	1 *l.*	or	1 *l.*
Australia	250			or	250 g.	1.125 *l.*	or	1.125 *l.*
Canada	200	and	50	and	200 g.	1.14 *l.*	or	1.14 *l.*
Ireland	200	or	50	or	250 g.	1 *l.*	and	2 *l.*
N. Zealand	200	or	50	or	250 g.	1.125 *l.*	and	4.5 *l*
S. Africa	400	and	50	and	250 g.	1 *l.*	and	2 *l.*
UK	200	or	50	or	250 g.	1 *l.*	and	2 *l.*

A non-resident may claim, free of duty and taxes, articles up to $100 in value for use as gifts for other people. This exemption is valid only if the gifts accompany you in your luggage, if you stay 72 hours or more, and have not claimed this exemption within the preceeding six months. Up to 100 cigars may be included within this gift exemption, but Cuban cigars are illegal.

Plants and foodstuffs also are subject to strict control; visitors from abroad may not import fruits, vegetables, or meat. The same goes for chocolates that contain liqueur.

Arriving and departing passengers are required to report any money or checks, etc., exceeding a total of $10,000.

E

ELECTRIC CURRENT

110-volt 60-cycle AC is standard throughout the US. Plugs are the flat, two- and three-pronged variety. Visitors from abroad will need a transformer (240–110V) and an adapter plug for their electric razors, etc, unless they are the dual-voltage type.

EMERGENCIES

Most cities and towns have a special 911 number for emergencies – fire, police, ambulance, and paramedics. Otherwise, dial '0' and the operator will connect you with the service you need.

G

GETTING TO THE USA

Scheduled flights: New York is the principal gateway to the US from the British Isles, but major transatlantic carriers offer direct flights from Heathrow and Gatwick to many other US destinations. Direct flights are also available from Ireland. Flying time from London to New York is 7 hours, to Los Angeles, 11 hours. From Sydney and Auckland, scheduled flights leave daily for Los Angeles, with connections to other US cities. Direct flights are also available to the United States from most other countries.

Aside from the standard first-class and economy fares, many other types of fares are available. Consult an airline or travel agency for the latest information about discounts and special fares.

Charter flights: Some are organized by scheduled airlines, others by special holiday companies. ABC (Advance Booking Charter) flights must be reserved at least 21 days in advance for a minimum stay of 7 days.

Package holidays: A wide variety are available, ranging from fully organized to flexible. Some packages include the rental cost of an RV (motorhome) or camping equipment.

Baggage: You are allowed to check in, free of charge, two suitcases of normal size on scheduled transatlantic flights. In addition, one piece of hand baggage of a size that fits easily under the aircraft seat may be carried on board. If in doubt, check size and weight restrictions with your travel agent or air carrier when booking your ticket.

It is advisable to insure all luggage for the duration of your trip. Any travel agent can make the necessary arrangements.

GETTING AROUND THE USA

By Car

Rental: Cars can be rented at airports and in most cities. Charges vary, so shop around for the best deal. Most car-rental companies offer a flat rate with unlimited mileage. If you are planning to drive more than 70 miles (112km) a day, this is probably the solution for you. There are also companies specializing in older (3 or 4 years), worn but mechanically sound, cars. They can be (not always) much less expensive and good for local touring. You may also want to look into rent-here, leave-there deals.

A major credit card is essential to avoid paying an enormous deposit; some companies even refuse to accept cash as a deposit. For tourists from non-English-speaking countries, a translation of your drivers license is highly recommended, together with the national license itself, or an International Driving Permit.

Auto driveaway: If you'd like a budget way to cross the country, look into an auto-driveaway deal. Several companies engage people to drive cars from one part of the country to a specified destination. A refundable security deposit and an International Driving Permit are required, and the driver must be at least 21 years old. You pay gasoline (petrol) expenses yourself, and you have to take a reasonably direct route established in advance. Consult the Yellow Pages of the telephone directory under 'Automobile Transporters & Driveaway Companies.'

American Automobile Association: The AAA offers lots of information on traveling in the US, as well as short-term insurance for visitors. The AAA also helps members, as well as foreign visitors affiliated with recognized automobile associations, in case of breakdown or other problems.

Contact AAA World Travel:
1000 AAA Drive, Heathrow, Florida 32746-5603
Tel: (1-800) AAA-HELP (222-4357)

On the road: Drive on the right. Intersections are generally marked with stop or yield signs to indicate who has priority. Speed limits, almost always posted, are strictly enforced, as are stop signs. Overtaking is legal on both sides on many major highways. An excellent interstate highway system crosses the US. Odd numbers designate highways running north–south, while even-numbered interstates run east–west.

Generally the speed limit on highways is 55mph (89km/h), but it can go up to 65mph (105km/h) on interstate highways in some states. In a few little-populated mountain and prairie states, experiments are being conducted where there is no speed limit at all. If in doubt, check locally.

If you have a breakdown on an expressway, pull over onto the right-hand shoulder, tie a handkerchief to the doorhandle or radio aerial, raise the hood (bonnet), and wait in the car for assistance. Use your hazard lights as well, day or night.

Gasoline (petrol) and services: Stations are numerous and easy to locate. Many stations might be closed in the evenings and on weekends. At night, some gas stations require exact change or a credit card. No tipping is required for 'full-service,' though the per-gallon price is often higher.

By Bus

Greyhound bus lines provide transportation to and from cities all over the United States. Passengers can make as many stopovers en route as they wish, provided the destination is reached before the ticket expires.

Sometimes travel by bus costs about the same – or even more – than flying; don't automatically assume the bus is less expensive. Flat-rate rover passes for specified periods of unlimited travel are available. These tickets must be purchased outside the US.

Greyhound: tel: (1-800) 231-2222.

By Train

Five hundred major cities and towns are linked daily by Amtrak, America's national railroad passenger corporation. Amtrak is currently advertising a variety of bargain fares, including excursion and family fares; the *USA Railpass*, the equivalent of the Eurailpass, can only be purchased abroad, but many package tours are available in the US. Trains are a far less efficient means of transportation than in Europe – buses are usually a better option for long-distance travel, though trains are more comfortable. Tel: (1-800) USA-RAIL.

By Air

Air travel is by far the quickest and most convenient way of getting around the US. Shuttle services operate on some heavily traveled routes, and with the emergence of 'paperless tickets,' traveling by air is as simple and straightforward as any other means of transportation. Fares change constantly, so it would be wise to consult an airline or travel agency for the latest information about discounts and special deals. Alternately, be on the look-out for special deals on the internet. Fares tend to be lowest during the wintertime.

Local Transportation

Municipal buses operate in most cities and towns, and the exact change is required. Some big cities have subway (underground rail) systems. Maps of the network are usually posted at every station and in every train, and can be obtained at the ticket booth in any station. To take the subway, you need a token or fare card (purchased at the booth), which you insert in the turnstile.

Taxis are lined up at airports, train stations, and bus terminals, or you can hail a cab in the street or telephone for one. A tip of at least 15 percent is expected. On arrival in the US, if you take a taxi from the airport into town, make sure you have several small banknotes (bills) – 20s are best – with you, as cab drivers will not give change for large denominations.

H

HEALTH AND MEDICAL CARE

Free medical service is not available in the US, and a visit to the doctor can be expensive, hospitalization an economic disaster. Holiday medical insurance is therefore a wise precaution. You can arrange for coverage through one of the big international companies or your travel agent.

Foreign visitors may wish to ask their consulate for a list of doctors. In an emergency, local telephone operators are an excellent source of advice (dial '0').

HITCHHIKING

Except on expressways and parkways it is legal to hitchhike – but not really advisable. The practice does not have a good reputation – there are too many stories of assault, robbery, and worse. As a result, Americans, usually a warm-hearted lot, are wary of picking up anybody, and you may find yourself waiting hours for a ride.

L

LIQUOR (ALCOHOL) REGULATIONS

Liquor laws vary a good deal from state to state and sometimes within a state. Utah is strictest, Nevada the most liberal. Some states allow alcohol to be sold in supermarkets or drugstores, in others only licensed liquor (or 'package') stores sell even beer. The sale of alcohol on Sundays and holidays (except by the glass in restaurants) is frequently restricted or prohibited.

The minimum age for purchasing or drinking alcoholic beverages in a public place ranges from 18 to 21, according to the state. You may be asked for some identification ('ID') when buying alcohol, whether or not you look under age, and you can be refused if you have no ID.

LOST PROPERTY

Air, rail, and bus terminals and many stores have 'lost-and-found' departments, and restaurants also put aside lost articles. If your lost property is valuable, contact the police. If you lose your passport, get in touch with your nearest consulate immediately.

M

MAPS

Tourist information authorities distribute free maps and brochures. City and state maps can be purchased in bookstores and stationery stores and at many gas stations and larger supermarkets.

MONEY MATTERS (See also CUSTOMS AND ENTRY REGULATIONS)

Currency: The dollar is divided into 100 cents.

Coins: 1 (penny), 5 (nickel), 10 (dime), 25 (quarter), 50 (half dollar), and $1.

Bills: $1, $2 (rare), $5, $10, $20, $50, and $100. Larger denominations ($500 and $1,000) are not in general circulation. All denominations are the same size and same green color. The newer $5, $10, $20, $50, and $100 bills are easier to read, but check each one before paying.

Currency exchange: Normal banking hours are from 9am to 3pm, Monday to Friday.

Only major banks in larger cities or at international airports will change foreign money or foreign-currency travelers' checks, so it's important to carry cash or travelers' checks in dollars. If you're cashing travelers' checks in a bank, be sure to take your passport. It's a good idea to always have a supply of $1–$10 bills on hand for taxis, tipping, and small purchases.

Credit cards: Credit cards play an even greater role here than in Europe. In the US, they are a way of life, and most Americans have several. The major credit cards are accepted almost everywhere. When paying for goods or services, including hotel and restaurant checks, you will usually be asked: 'Cash or charge?,' meaning you have the choice of paying either in cash or in 'plastic money'.

Travelers' checks: Visitors from abroad will find travelers' checks drawn on American banks, or the easily obtainable checks issued by American Express, far easier to deal with than those issued by local banks. Travelers' checks are widely accepted in stores, restaurants, and hotels. Only carry small amounts of cash at a time, and, if possible, keep the balance of your checks in the hotel safe.

ATMS: These are widely available. However, most banks charge non-depositors a small fee to use their machines.

N

NATIONAL PARKS

Government-protected reserves, found all over the US, take in everything from stretches of coastland and wayside campgrounds to wildlife reserves and wilderness areas. The sites designated 'National Park' or 'National Monument' are areas of outstanding historical, geological, and scenic importance. Almost all can be reached by car or bus, and some have direct connections to major cities by rail or air.

Each state also has numerous 'State Parks,' generally of lesser consequence although many have outstanding scenic and recreational resources.

High season is mid-July to mid-August, when the most popular parks are likely to be crowded and advance reservations for campgrounds recommended. Park rangers often provide guided tours and usually schedule organized summer and winter activities. Entrance fees to the parks vary. The reasonably priced *Golden*

Eagle Passport (buy it inside the park) entitles all the occupants of a private car to unlimited access to national parks. Seniors are entitled to reduced rates.

A few of the greatest parks have been dealt with in detail in this guide. Here are a few more:

Bryce Canyon National Park (Utah): A fantasy land of pink cliffs, dramatic rock formations, and breathtaking scenery.

Mesa Verde National Park (Colorado): Native Americans abandoned this prehistoric 'green tabletop' 800 years ago, leaving behind stone cities built into the cliffside.

Petrified Forest National Park (Arizona): In the most colorful area of the Painted Desert, six forests of fallen logs, 200 million years old, have turned into jasper and agate.

Shenandoah National Park (Virginia): Nearest wilderness park to the nation's capital, this park consists of a 105-mile (170-km) stretch of wooded Blue Ridge Mountains.

For further information, write to the Department of the Interior, National Park Service, 1849 C Street NW, Washington, DC. 20240; tel: (202) 208-4747 (or go to <www.nps.gov>). For state parks, write to the state tourist department or do a search on the web.

P

PHOTOGRAPHY AND VIDEO

All popular brands of film and photographic equipment are available. Try to buy in discount stores, where prices are reduced. Color-print film takes 1 hour to 5 days to be developed, black-and-white film and transparencies up to a week.

POLICE (See also CRIME AND THEFT and EMERGENCIES)

City police are concerned with local crime and traffic violations, while Highway Patrol officers (also called State Troopers) ensure road safety, and are on the lookout for people speeding or driving under the influence of alcohol or drugs.

American police officers are often fair and friendly. Do not hesitate to approach any unbusy officer and ask for assistance or information. In case of emergency, find a phone, dial '911' or '0,' and ask the operator to contact the police.

PRICES

The US has a larger range of prices for any one item than you will find anywhere else, as well as a greater choice. The best prices are usually in the huge discount houses, located just off highways and in suburban areas. Independent gas stations charge less than those run by the large oil companies. Prices often do not include a state sales tax (normally 4 to 9 percent) and a city or resort tax.

PUBLIC HOLIDAYS

The following public holidays are – with a few exceptions – celebrated nationwide. For an explantion of *, see the next page.

New Year's Day	January 1
Martin Luther King Day*	Third Monday in January
Presidents Day**	Third Monday in February
Memorial Day	Last Monday in September
Independence Day	July 4
Labor Day	First Monday in September
Columbus Day***	Second Monday in October
Veteran's Day	November 11
Thanksgiving	Fourth Thursday in November
Christmas	December 25

* celebrated in most states; on January 15 in a few states

** celebrated on February 22 in some states (also called Washington's Birthday or Washington-Lincoln Day)

*** celebrated in most states, on October 12 in some states (also called Pioneer's Day, Farmers' Day, Fraternal Day, Discoverer's Day)

Lincoln's Birthday (February 12) is sometimes observed in the northern states, Robert E. Lee's Birthday (January19) and Confederate Memorial Day (late April/early May) is sometimes celebrated in southern states.

If a holiday falls on a Sunday, banks and most stores close on the following day. There are also long weekends (such as the one following Thanksgiving) when offices are closed for four days. Many restaurants never shut, however, not even at Christmas.

R

RADIO AND TELEVISION

You'll almost certainly have radio and television in your hotel room, with a vast choice of programs. Some television networks broadcast from 6am until 3 or 4am the next morning; others never go off the air. American commercial television aims to appeal to the largest possible number, while independent programmers like HBO and Fox-TV have some of the best and most original shows. The non-commercial Public Broadcasting Service (PBS) screens music and drama programs (many of them bought from the BBC) along with its own news and information broadcasts.

There are numerous AM and FM radio stations. Most broadcast pop or country music, but each large city has at least one classical-music radio station and some have jazz stations. Highest quality programming (including news) is generally on National Public Radio (NPR) stations.

RESTAURANTS

In the US, there's something for every taste and budget. You can dine in the luxurious surroundings of a fashionable restaurant or eat on the run at an informal lunch counter.

Away from major cities or metropolitain centers, however, special or restricted diets such as wheat or dairy-free, or even vegetarian, can be hard to satisfy.

Coffee shops and cafeterias: These offer sandwiches, hamburgers, salads, simple hot dishes, and pastries. They do not usually serve alcoholic drinks.

Delicatessens: Delis are a cross between grocery stores and restaurants (some are just restaurants), and are known for their gargantuan sandwiches. Other specialties include salads and hearty soups. Some delicatessens are kosher.

Diners: Originally a sort of coffee-shop-on-the-road built in the shape of a railroad dining car, some have now become quite elaborate and serve alcohol. But they're still open long (often 24) hours.

Fast-food outlets: You'll see plenty of reminders that you're in the land of McDonald's and Kentucky Fried Chicken. These are easy to find with their huge neon signs. However there are many chains that foreign visitors may never have heard of.

Health-food restaurants and juice bars: Every imaginable kind of fruit and vegetable juice is served here, as well as delicious salads, whole-food, and vegetarian specialties. Ingredients are often organic.

Pizzerias: These are great for a quick meal, and the pizzas are usually big enough for three people. You can also buy by the slice.

Take-outs: Small stores where you can order sandwiches, salads, assorted groceries, and drinks to take out and consume elsewhere. These are particularly good for picnic food.

RESTROOMS

Americans use the terms 'restroom,' 'powder room,' 'bathroom' (private) and 'ladies' or 'men's room' to indicate the toilet. If you encounter a pay-toilet, the usual charge is 25¢.

T

TIME ZONES AND DATES

The 48 contiguous states of the US are – from east to west – divided into four time zones: Eastern (GMT -5 hours), Central (-6), Mountain

(-7), and Pacific (-8). The major part of Alaska is on GMT -9 hours, and Hawaii ia on GMT -10. Under Daylight Saving Time, observed in all states but Arizona, Hawaii, and parts of Indiana, clocks move ahead one hour the first Sunday in April and turn back again the last Sunday in October.

TIPPING

In general, a service charge is not included in the bill; you are expected to tip the waiter, waitress, or bartender about 15 percent (more in luxury establishments). Movie house or theater ushers are not tipped, but doormen, cloakroom attendants, etc., should be remunerated – never less than a quarter.

Here are some more tipping suggestions:

Bell hop (porter)	50¢–$1 per bag (min. $1)
Hotel maid (not for single night)	$1 per day or $5 per week
Restroom attendant	50¢
Taxi driver	15 percent
Bus tour guide	10–15 percent
Hairdresser/barber	15 percent

TOURIST INFORMATION CENTERS

Convention and visitors bureaus in principal cities:

Atlanta: Convention and Visitors Bureau, 233 Peachtree Street, NE, Suite 100 Atlanta, GA 30303, tel: (404) 521-6600; <www.acvb.com>
Baltimore: Visitors Information Center, 100 Light Street, tel: (410) 659-7300 or (800) 343-3468; <www.baltimore.org>
Boston: Greater Boston Convention and Visitors Bureau, Two Copley Place, Suite 105, Boston, MA 02116, tel: (617) 536-4100; <www.bostonusa.com>
Chicago: Office of Tourism, 78 East Washington, Chicago, IL 60602, tel: (312) 744-2390; <www.877chicago.com>
Dallas: Convention and Visitors Bureau, 325 West St Paul Street, Dallas, TX 75201, tel: (214) 571-1000; <www.visitdallas.com>

Denver: Metro Convention and Visitors Bureau, 1555 California Street, Suite 300, Denver, CO 80202, tel: (303) 892-1112; <www.denver.org>

Detroit: Metro Convention and Visitors Bureau, 211 West Fort Street, Suite 1000, Detroit, MI 48226, tel: (313) 202-1952; <www.visitdetroit.com>

Houston: Greater Houston Convention and Visitors Bureau, 901 Bagby, Houston, TX 77002, tel: (713) 437-5267; <www.spacecity-usa.com>

Las Vegas: Convention and Visitors Authority, 3150 Paradise Road, Las Vegas, NV 89109, tel: (702) 892-7663; <www.vegasfreedom. com>

Los Angeles: Greater Los Angeles Visitors and Convention Bureau, 633 West 5th Street, tel: (213) 624-7300; <www.lacvb.com>

Miami/Miami Beach: Miami Convention and Visitors Bureau, 701 Brickell Avenue, Miami, FL 33131, tel: (305) 539-3084; <www.tropicoolmiami.com>

New Orleans: New Orleans Metropolitan Convention and Visitors Bureau, 1520 Sugar Bowl Drive, New Orleans, LA 70112, tel: (504) 566-5019; <www.nomcvb.com>

New York: Convention and Visitors Bureau, 810 Seventh Avenue (at 53rd Sreet) New York, NY 10019, tel: (212) 397-8222; <www.nycvisit.com>

Philadelphia: Convention and Visitors Bureau, Suite 2020, 1515 Market Sreet, Philadelphia, PA 19102, tel: (215) 636-3320; <www.pcvb.com>

Phoenix: Convention and Visitors Bureau, 1 Arizona Center, 400 East. Van Buren Street, Suite 600 Phoenix, AZ 85004, tel: (602) 452-6252; <www.visitphoenix.com>

Salt Lake: Convention and Visitors Bureau, 90 South West Temple, Salt Lake City, UT 84101, tel: (801) 521-2822; <www.visitsaltlake. com>

San Antonio: Convention and Visitors Bureau, 203 South Street, Mary's Street, 2nd floor, TX 78298, tel: (210) 270-6700; <www.sanantoniocvb.com>

San Diego: Visitors Bureau, 401 B Street, Suite 1400, San Diego, CA 92101, tel: (619) 232-3100; <www.sandiego.org>

San Francisco: Visitor Information Center, 201 3rd Street, San Francisco, CA 94103, tel: (415) 227-2603; <www.sfvisitor.org>

Santa Fe: Convention and Visitors Bureau, Box 909, Santa Fe, NM 87504-0909, tel: (505) 955-6200; <www.santafe.org>

Seattle: Convention and Visitors Bureau, 520 Pike Street, Suite 1300, Seattle, WA 98101, tel: (206) 461-5815; <www.seeseattle.org>

Washington, DC: Convention and Visitors Association, 1212 New York Avenue, NW, Suite 600 Washington, DC 20005, tel: (202) 789-7046; <www.washington.org>

W

WEIGHTS, MEASURES, AND CLOTHING SIZES

The United States is one of the last countries in the world to resist the metric system. Milk and fruit juice are sold by the quart or half gallon, but wine and spirits now come in liter bottles. Food products usually have the weight marked in kilos and grams as well as pounds and ounces.

There are some differences between British and American measures: 1 US gallon = .833 Imperial gallon = 3.8 liters and 1 US quart = .833 Imperial quart = .9 liters.

Clothing sizes: women's dresses and suits

USA	8	10	12	14	16
UK	10	12	14	16	18
Continental	40	42	44	46	48

Note: Men's suit sizes are the same in the US and the UK. Continental sizes are 10 numerals higher, ie, US34, Continental 44.

INDEX

Berlitz

Discover the World, Speak the Language

With more than 40 million copies sold worldwide, Berli▮
Pocket Guides are renowned for their trustworth▮
coverage and remarkable portability. And, if you're eve▮
stuck for words, the equally portable Berlitz Phrase Book▮
have the answers in 33 languages, from Arabic to Swahi▮

www.berlitzpublishing.co▮